FORENSIC SIGNATURE EXAMINATION

About the Author

Steven A. Slyter is a forensic document examiner, and a past president of the Association of Forensic Document Examiners. He maintains a private practice in Louisville, Kentucky. His clients include attorneys, individuals, businesses, banks, security companies, and government offices. He has been recognized as a qualified questioned document expert in state and federal courts since 1973, and has made well over 100 court appearances in which he has given testimony relating to signature and handwriting authenticity, forgery identification, disguised writings, indented writings, typewriter identification, anonymous letters, graffiti, age of documents or writings, and alteration to documents. Mr. Slyter served for three years as Technical Editor of the *Journal of the Association of Forensic Document Examiners.* He has published numerous articles in the AFDE Journal. He has also published articles on document photography in STUDIO magazine. In 1995, Mr. Slyter's article "The Effects of Alterations to Documents" was published in Volume No. 29 of *American Jurisprudence,* PROOF OF FACTS, Third Series.

FORENSIC SIGNATURE EXAMINATION

By

STEVEN A. SLYTER
Certified Document Examiner

CHARLES C THOMAS • PUBLISHER
Springfield • Illinois • U.S.A.

Published and Distributed Throughout the World by

CHARLES C THOMAS • PUBLISHER
2600 South First Street
Springfield, Illinois 62794-9265

ISBN 0-398-06541-1 (cloth)
ISBN 0-398-06542-X (paper)

Library of Congress Catalog Card Number: 95-18290

With THOMAS BOOKS *careful attention is given to all details of manufacturing and design. It is the Publisher's desire to present books that are satisfactory as to their physical qualities and artistic possibilities and appropriate for their particular use.* THOMAS BOOKS *will be true to those laws of quality that assure a good name and good will.*

Printed in the United States of America
SC-R-3

Library of Congress Cataloging-in-Publication Data

Slyter, Steven A.
Forensic signature examination / by Steven A. Slyter.
p. cm.
Includes bibliographical references and index.
ISBN 0-398-06541-1 (cloth) — ISBN 0-398-06542-X (pbk.)
1. Writing—Identification. 2. Signatures (Writing) 3. Legal documents—Identification. 4. Evidence, Expert. 5. Forgery. 6. Graphology. I. Title.
HV8074.S59 1995
363.2'562—dc20 95-18290
CIP

Dedicated to My Children
Monica, Pamela and Matthew

INTRODUCTION

"This can't be right!" The client leans forward across the desk, the tone is serious with undercurrents of puzzlement and anger. The document pushed forward is of great importance to this person. A lot is at stake now—money, reputations, memories of a loved one, careers, the future, even someone's freedom . . . critical questions must be addressed; "Is this a valid signature? Or, is it a forgery?" A handwriting expert must be hired to search for the answers.

From this opening meeting through to the final resolution of the issues which are raised by the document in question, the specialized knowledge and skills of the handwriting expert will be needed if the truth is to be found. The pathway through a questioned document case does not lie in a straight line. There will be expected and unexpected twists, turns, and obstacles to navigate before the expert's work is finished. At many points in a case an expert will find the evidence confusing. It is easy to head off down a dead end path and have to backup to reestablish the direction of the investigation.

The most valuable tool with which to meet any navigation problem is a solid, well known, unmoving, distant point of reference. My own favorite aid to navigation is a prayer which, though probably thousands of years old, might just as well have been written today with the forensic expert in mind.

> From the cowardice that shrinks from new truth—
> From the laziness that is contented with half-truths—
> From the arrogance that thinks it knows all truth—
> Oh, God of Truth, deliver us.
>
> Anonymous Jewish Prayer

When setting out to become a document examiner, having a distant point by which to steer is vital. However, setting a course by focusing on that goal is easier than getting started on the trip. A document examiner may be called upon to address a wide range of questions relating to the purported history of the production and storage of critical documents.

In addition to handwriting and signature comparisons, the document examiner must be knowledgeable of inks, paper, copy machines, typing machines, indeed any process that might relate to documents.

Some experts working on questioned documents have specialized. There are experts who work almost exclusively on questions of typewriter identification or paper and ink chemistry. For most questioned document examiners a question of signature authenticity is the central issue in more than 90 percent of their cases. How does one start to build the body of knowledge necessary to become a document examiner? Start right here. There is nothing more important to the examination of questioned documents than effective, objective skills for forensic signature examination.

I began my studies toward becoming a handwriting expert in 1970. In my twenty-five years of direct involvement, and in my reading of the literature from decades before, precious little has been done to develop objective paradigms for the analysis of signature habits. While 90 percent of the document examiner's work involves signatures, more than 90 percent of the progress in terms of tools and techniques for the document examiner has been in laboratory devices for testing the physical parameters of documents.

Testing for such things as infrared luminescence of ink or indentations in a sheet of paper is wonderfully objective work. There are certain pieces of equipment which must be used and certain procedures to be followed. Anyone conducting the tests correctly will arrive at the same results. The methods and equipment that have been developed are invaluable in those cases in which they are needed. It is understandable that so much attention has been given to physical testing. When cases involving evidence gained through such testing require a court appearance the document examiner can enjoy the luxury of testifying to demonstrable facts. The jury seeing the results of physical tests is willing to view the document examiner as a scientist. By its nature, signature examination is not so scientific.

Signatures are relied upon for identification because they are unique. For our own subjective reasons each of us develops habits of pen movement which come to represent our signature. It has appeared to some outspoken critics that handwriting experts have been equally subjective in forming opinions about the authenticity of signatures. Whether due to spin-control journalism, sound-bite news, say-anything talk shows, or better education—jurors seem to be less willing to accept "I say so" testimony. Today, anyone who appears in court as a paid witness must expect to be viewed with skepticism.

In the desire to persuade jurors, I believe that many experts have made a poor choice of strategies. Too many experts try to paint themselves as a combination high-priest and magician, in possession of some complex special knowledge that would be far beyond the grasp of mere mortal jurors. The worst of these offer condescending testimony along the line of " . . . my experience makes me terribly important, so just trust me."

When experts act as magicians they discount the value of their own work and insult the jury. If signature examination is not science—neither is it magic. It is a technical discipline. The best experts employ the scientific method in a systematic, objective search for the truth. I doubt that any of us would want our fate decided by a juror who believes that David Copperfield made the Statue of Liberty disappear. Why then would we want a juror to believe there is something magical about signature comparison? What is magic to one person is a technology to another. There is a critical difference between magicians and technicians. Using unambiguous language, the technician will gladly explain how the feat was accomplished.

By defining the parameters that guide an examination of signatures an examiner can avoid any appearance of nonobjective work. Before the case is accepted and any examination of documents begins, a competent examiner should be willing and able to define what will be compared; how the elements which will be compared relate to one another; the thresholds of significance in matching and mismatching elements; how decisions will be made about any differences that might be found; and the critical criteria for forming an opinion. No one can question the skills of an athlete who calls a shot before the action begins. Likewise, the expert whose working methods and decision-making parameters are consistently applied to every case cannot be charged with subjectivity.

One of the earmarks of a science is that it is alive and changing, always growing on what has come before. Document examiners too often view the works of founders such as Albert S. Osborn as the final word on the subject rather than an inspired beginning. In this book I explain working parameters and systems which I have developed in my own practice. These developments grew from my studies and application of the principles published by the pioneers in handwriting identification. In my own practice these tools have been used daily for many years and I have found them to be useful and effective. I hope and fully believe, that these tools can be as useful for others.

ACKNOWLEDGMENTS

The ideas and methods presented in this book have been under development and revision for more than a dozen years. I am grateful to the many friends and colleagues who contributed to this process. They have listened, offered constructive criticism, and given needed encouragement.

A document examiner works in the advocacy system. There is never a shortage of criticism. Some of the critics have not intended their remarks to be constructive. However, I have always recognized that they put a lot of thought and energy into finding any weak spot in my work. They have certainly helped me develop stronger tools.

I am grateful to Monica Hall and Jean Yingling for their assistance in editing this work. They were most helpful.

Finally, this book would not have been possible without the support and assistance of Nancy H. Cole, Questioned Document Examiner in Palo Alto, California. From the beginning, Nancy has patiently read and edited countless pages. She has helped me to bury some bad ideas and she nurtured better ideas through difficult times. Nancy, thank you.

CONTENTS

FORENSIC SIGNATURE EXAMINATION

Chapter One

AN OVERVIEW OF SIGNATURE IDENTIFICATION

Many document examination problems present the examiner with a straightforward question of fact. Such questions may include: Was this document altered? Were these pages prepared on the same paper? . . . with the same ink? These questions can be answered objectively with demonstrable, physical laboratory tests, and, when necessary, the examiner can be called to testify to the results.

Questions of signature identification, however, cannot be answered with such purely objective, scientific clarity. The handwriting expert must rely on special knowledge, skills, and experience to reach an honest opinion. Document examiners working with questions of handwriting identification face an ironic task. They call on techniques and skills from many of the physical sciences and base their work on the scientific method; yet, it is the very subjectivity of handwriting which makes it society's most important and most prevalent form of identification.

There is nothing unique about investigating a case in which a signature is a part of the evidence. There is often a desire to equate signature comparisons with fingerprint identification. Signatures change due to many intentional and unintentional influences. A more accurate analogy can be drawn between signature identification and physical identification.

"Blue eyes" would not be a sufficient description to identify a suspect. That descriptor would be one element in a body of information which, collectively, would establish identity. In a similar sense, handwriting habits can be viewed as elemental descriptors. These elements combine into the more complex and significant aspects of rhythm (the many aspects of how the pen is moved) and form (the designs created in the writing). It is the final, integrated *balance* of rhythm and form which, in total, is sufficiently individualized to be reliable for identification.

When building the foundation for a physical identification, an investigator needs to define a large enough combination of descriptors that the subject might be distinguished from the group. For example, blond hair and a visible birth mark might be added to the blue-eyes description. The individuality of the information and the size of the group (universe of possible suspects) will determine whether an identification might be possible. The situation is the same for the identification of handwriting.

Just as an investigator would search for all the details that might assist in a physical identification, anyone investigating a signature should also try to establish as many details as possible early in the investigation. Even before a document examiner is retained, the investigators need to gather as much information as possible for the record.

Original documents should be secured. The statements of any parties who might have information relating to the origin or safe keeping of key documents should be preserved. And, just as in a physical search, when it is believed that a signature has been forged, it is important to develop a basis for defining the universe of possible suspects—or more accurately, the universe of possible writers.

The nature of the case and the size of the universe of possible writers will help define the requirements for gathering exemplar materials. Exemplars, also referred to as standards or known writings, are the materials presented to the document examiner as the known or acknowledged *true writings* of each subject. Exemplars might be gathered from normal course of business writings, they might be produced at the examiner's request or both. The document examiner's work begins with a brief review of the questioned signature and then moves on to the more detailed examination of the exemplars.

Any collection of a subject's exemplar signatures will show that each element of the writing varies slightly from signature to signature. For example, some parts of the signature might show slight differences of slant or design from one signature to the next. The extent of these variations is small for some writers and quite extensive for others. The document examiner must assemble sufficient exemplar materials to be satisfied that collectively they present a fair and reasonable definition of the subject's range of normal variation. A detailed definition of a subject's writing habits must be developed before the examiner has a basis for testing the elements displayed in the questioned signature. Only after normal variations have been defined by the exemplar collection can any variations seen in the questioned signature be given their proper weight.

It is obvious that for handwriting to be useful, the designs used for the letters and numbers must be conventional enough to be recognized.

That is less true for signatures. It is not unusual for signatures to include designs that are not part of any generally accepted writing system. Many people use a slant, size, or style of writing when producing their signature which is quite different from their general writing habits.[1]

A question relating to the authenticity of a signature is the problem most frequently brought to a document examiner. In these cases the circumstance surrounding the document may be unique, but the critical question to be addressed in the examination is the same. *Does this questioned signature (Q) match the known, true signatures (K) of this subject?* In other words, does Q equal K?

This book limits the discussion of examination of writing habits to the examination of signatures. Signatures are the critical issue in most document examination cases. The methods of examination and comparison for signatures presented here also apply to the examination of handwritings. Handwriting, numbers, and printing are examined with essentially the same steps necessary for the examination of signatures. By beginning with a study of signature examination, it is easier to grasp and master the techniques involved. Anyone who has practiced and mastered the processes of signature comparisons will have little difficulty extending their studies to include other writings.

The following chapters offer the reader a systematic method for learning and practicing the skills of forensic signature examination. The tools offered do not apply only to selected examples: they can be applied to the forensic study of any signature—that is their purpose.

I have chosen to limit the use of illustrations in this book in the belief that readers will gain more by applying these tools to their own collections of signatures. If a picture is worth a thousand words, firsthand experience is worth a thousand pictures. Forensic signature examination is a discipline learned through practice. Applying these tools to even one collection of signatures will be of benefit to the reader.

Before going on to the following chapters, gather together a dozen of your own canceled checks. Cut the signatures from these checks and glue them to a sheet of stiff paper. If you do not wish to cut the signatures from your checks make high quality copies of them and cut the signatures from the copies. When you have assembled your signature study board, make several high quality copies. As you read further you will be able to use these copies to test and practice what is presented.

---

[1]From Hilton, O., *Scientific Examination of Questioned Documents*, ©1992 by Ordway Hilton, CRC Press, Boca Raton, Florida, publisher. With permission. p. 173.

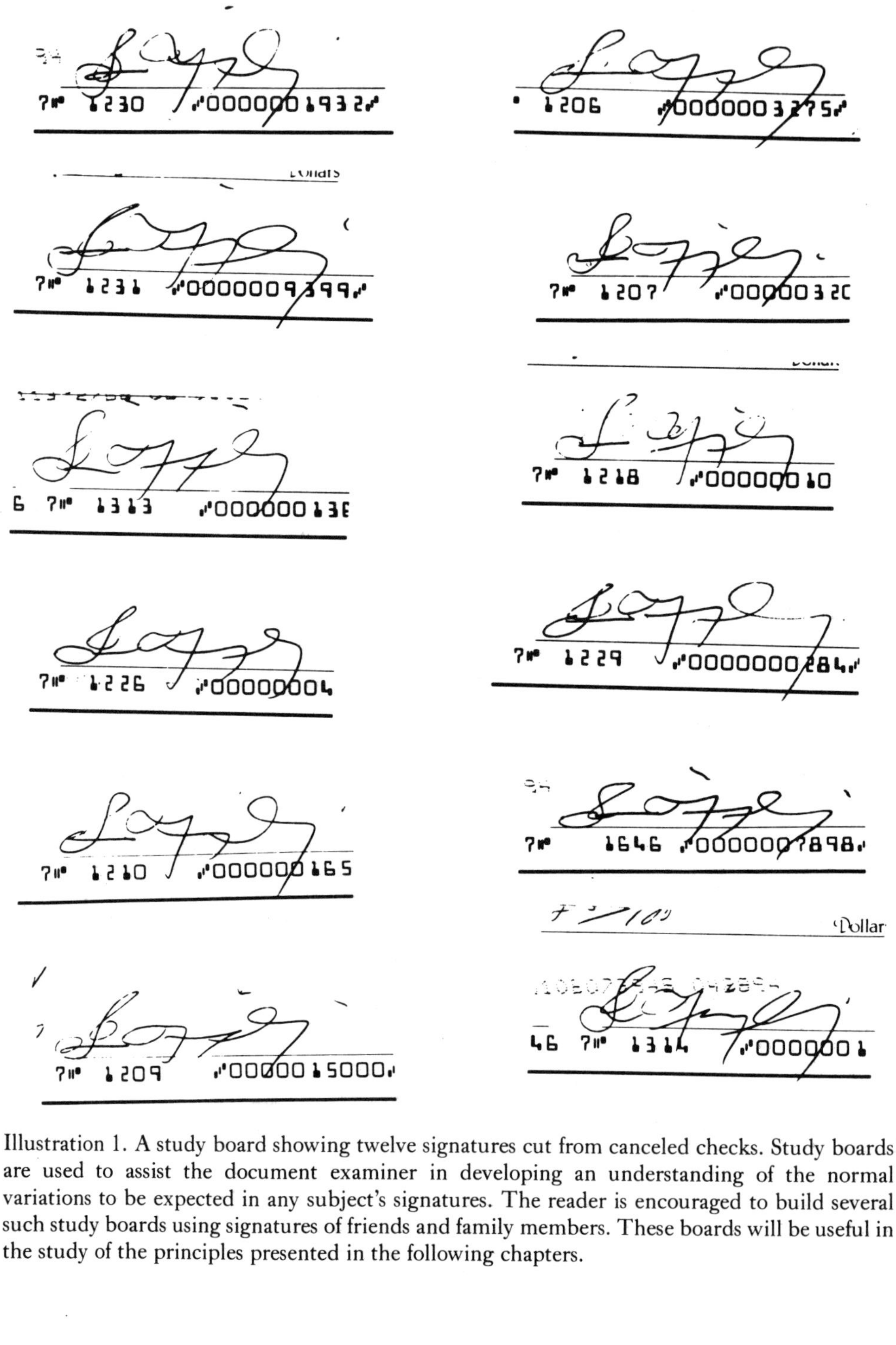

Illustration 1. A study board showing twelve signatures cut from canceled checks. Study boards are used to assist the document examiner in developing an understanding of the normal variations to be expected in any subject's signatures. The reader is encouraged to build several such study boards using signatures of friends and family members. These boards will be useful in the study of the principles presented in the following chapters.

Chapter Two

SIGNATURES

Signatures are produced by force of habit. Once the writer begins to sign, habit dictates the intricate movements of the pen. The hand moves in a personalized pattern of writing rhythms as the characters are formed. Pen speed, the proportions of each movement, and the subtleties of pen pressure are dynamically balanced without conscious effort, as the designs of the signature are formed. In a genuine signature, unconscious integration of these elements of pen movement produces a unique balance of rhythm and form.

The critical consideration in the forensic examination of signatures is this balance of the impulses controlling the movements of the pen and the intricacies of the forms created. Only automatic, unconscious force of habit can keep the whole, complex activity in dynamic balance. If a forged signature is to have a reasonable chance of being accepted as genuine, the forger must imitate both the form and the rhythmic flow of the victim's true signature.[2]

When someone attempts to imitate a signature it does not flow from unconscious habit. When effort is focused on the forms, rhythm suffers. And, if conscious effort is focused on imitating natural writing rhythm, the accuracy in matching the forms of the characters suffers. For the great majority of subjects, the balance of pen rhythms and character designs cannot be imitated by conscious effort. In Albert S. Osborn's words, "Developed, natural writing is an almost automatic act and follows the fixed grooves of habit, but as soon as attention is given to it, it necessarily becomes strained and unnatural."[3]

The key principle underlying the practice of signature identification is that only habit can keep the pen moving at a uniquely individualized, dynamic rhythm/form balance. An imitation is detectable when the writer makes an error of rhythm or form, which causes the false signa-

[2]Harrison, Wilson R.: *Forgery Detection, A Practical Guide.* New York, Frederick A. Praeger, 1964, p. 107.

[3]Osborn, Albert S.: *Questioned Documents,* Second Edition. Chicago, Nelson-Hall Co., 1929, p. 274.

ture to differ significantly from the range of normal variation defined by the victim's exemplars.

Handwriting experts are frequently asked whether they can *prove* that a questioned signature was written by an individual. Unless the examiner actually witnessed the materials being produced, he cannot claim to *prove* who produced it. Signature examination, like any other scientific inquiry, is a process by which a thoughtfully designed hypothesis is put to a series of tests. An hypothesis is a positive statement for which tests can be devised to determine whether it is valid.

As at the outset of any scientific experiment, the document examiner must define the hypothesis, or clearly state the exact purpose of the examination. It is impossible to prove a negative: therefore, the hypothesis must be expressed as a positive statement. Taking a questioned signature (Q1) and one set of exemplars at a time (K1, K2, K3, . . . etc.), the document examiner always works to test the same hypothetical statement.

For every forensic signature examination the key hypothesis is: "the writer of these exemplars is also the writer of this questioned material".

Several axioms follow the key hypothesis. Axioms are statements which must be true if the fundamental hypothesis is true. In this application of the scientific method, for the key hypothesis, "The writer of the signatures in exemplar set K1 is also the writer of the questioned signature Q1," the axioms which would follow are:

- The speed at which the pen was moved when signing Q1 is within the range of variations in pen speed defined by the signatures in Set K1.
- The proportions of the pen movements in Q1 are within the range of variation of proportions defined by Set K1.
- The pressure and pressure changes on the pen when signing Q1 is within the range of variation in pen pressure defined by the signatures in Set K1.
- The designs of the characters in Q1 are within the range of variation in designs defined by the signatures in Set K1.
- And the critical axiom—the dynamic, rhythm/form balance in signature Q1 is not significantly different from the range of variation in rhythm/form balance defined by the signatures in Set K1.

There can be legitimate reasons why someone's genuine signature does not equal his or her usual signature habits. In recognition of that possibility, there is one further axiom to consider.

• If signature Q1 is significantly different from the signatures in Set K1 then there is an acceptable explanation for that difference.

That key hypothesis and the six axioms which follow, form the basic skeleton for every signature examination. Provided with an adequate supply of reliable exemplar signatures, the examiner who systematically works out the answer to each of the six axioms will be led to the correct response (true or false) to the key hypothesis.

The document examiner does not "prove" that the signature in question is by the writer of K1 or that a questioned document is genuine. Neither is it proven that a signature is forged. An examiner's expertise and familiarity with the scientific process qualifies the expert to express a professional *opinion* as to whether the stated hypothesis is supported, or not supported, by the tests conducted.

When a questioned signature shows a significant, inexplicable difference of rhythm and/or form than that which is defined by an adequate body of the subject's exemplars, the examiner must conclude that the subject did not produce the questioned signature. Correctly stated, "the hypothesis that the signatures in Set K1 and subject Q1 were written by the same person is not supported by the measurements and comparisons carried out."[4]

---

[4]Harrison, Wilson R. M.Sc., Ph.D.: *Suspect Documents, Their Scientific Examination.* Chicago, Nelson-Hall, 1981, p. 343.

Chapter Three

ELEMENTS OF COMPARISON

In instructors' presentations and in experts' testimony, the subject of forensic signature examination has been difficult to understand. This has been due to the lack of a structured system for explaining the interrelationships of the elements involved in producing a signature. It is arguable that the final integration of movements that make a signature unique cannot be quantified. Nonetheless, it is useful to this study and to the analysis of signatures, to identify the elements involved and study how these elements combine.

Handwriting habits can be defined at the elemental level. These simple, measurable elements combine into more complex and more significant aspects of rhythm and form. Ultimately, it is only the final, integrated *balance* of rhythm and form which is sufficiently individualized to be reliable for identification.

Handwriting, and especially signatures, present a balance between the rhythm of the pen movements, and the design of the forms created. The relationships of the elements of this balance can be diagramed as follows in Figure 1.

These interrelationships of handwriting elements form a basis for the forensic analysis of signature habits. It is the final *BALANCE* of rhythm and form which is CRITICAL in signature comparisons, not simply the matching of individual elements.

Rhythm

The chart in Figure 1 shows the two PRIMARY aspects of writing—rhythm and form. Of the two, rhythm is the more difficult to analyze and explain. Lawyers, judges, jurors, and even a few document examiners look only at forms when comparing signatures.[5] This limited view can lead to errors since, of the two (rhythm and form), rhythm

[5]Osborn, pp. 284–285.

ELEMENTS OF COMPARISON

Interrelationships of Handwriting Variables

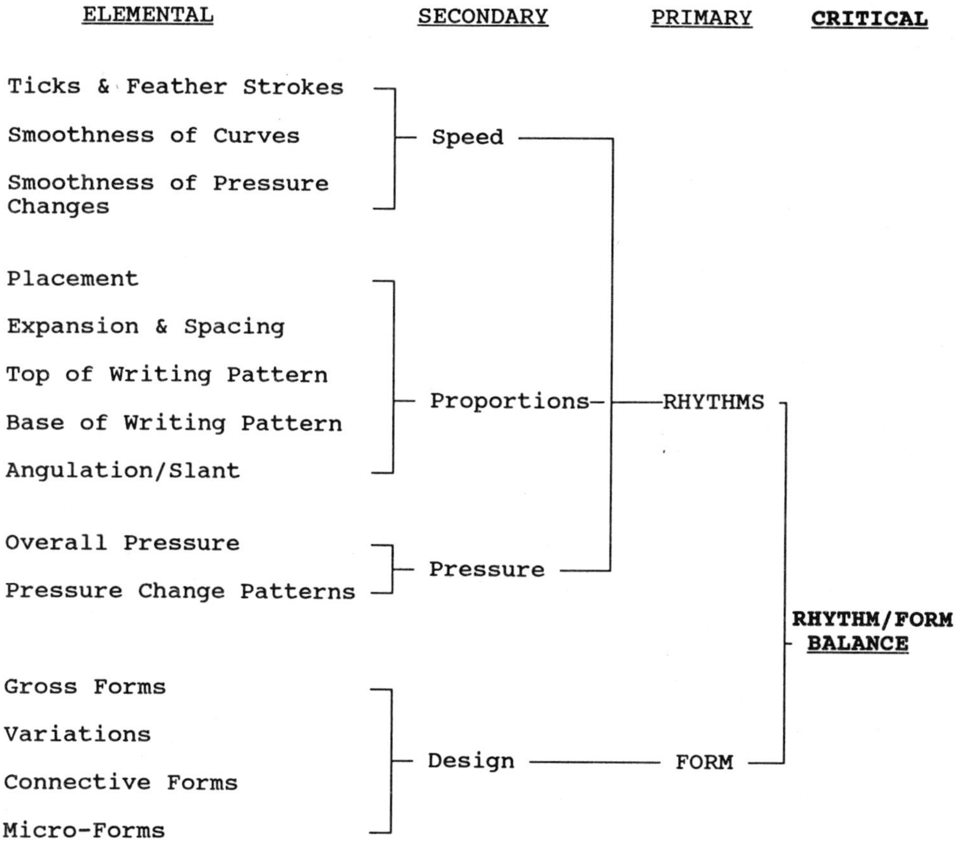

The hypothesis that the signatures being examined were produced by the same person is supported when the CRITICAL BALANCE of Rhythm and Form in the subject sample is within the range of variation defined by the exemplar samples - with the absence of any significant, inexplicable difference.

Figure 1.

involves the more subtle habits and is the more difficult aspect to imitate. Just as rhythm ties notes together creating music instead of noise, it is the rhythm in a signature that gives it integrated flow and individuality.

Some examiners speak of rhythm only when a writing shows a smooth flow of pen movements. They may speak of "good line quality" in a writing with smoothly integrated rhythms. For others, if they mention rhythm at all, it is as a vague, unexplainable phenomena which is only present in legible or pleasing signatures.

Some writers are able to integrate writing impulses well and their writing will be pleasing to the eye. Others are not able to integrate writing impulses smoothly and produce a writing which may be erratic and difficult to read. The skill with which the writer integrates movements might be described with any number of adjectives. Writing rhythm might be described as fluid, halting, broken, highly regular, highly variable, artistic, crude as having good (or poor) line quality, and so forth. Regardless of what adjectives best fit, every writing is constructed from writing impulses and thus exhibits some level of rhythm—which any would-be imitator must attempt to match.[6]

The dynamics of rhythm make it possible to see the same identity in a signature, whether it is written on a small note or across a large chalkboard, just as you would recognize the same music, whether it is played loudly, softly, or badly.

The analysis of signatures begins with the analysis of the elements of rhythm. Every writing has rhythm, indeed every writing is produced by a complex combination of many rhythms. Every movement of the pen—up, down, left, right—combined with the vertical movement which is seen as a change of pen pressure, is the product of a writing impulse.[7] In Figure 1 the rhythm of the pen movement is broken down into the SECONDARY aspects of Speed of the writing; the relative Proportions of the movements; and the regulation of Pressure on the writing instrument. Each of the SECONDARY aspects of rhythm is composed of several ELEMENTAL considerations.

In each person's signature, the elements of rhythm will move through a range of normal variations. A collection of anyone's signatures will show some written a little faster, some a little slower, some larger, and some smaller, etc. Forensic signature analysis requires the analysis of a sufficient number of exemplars to satisfy the examiner that they provide a basis for reaching a fair and reasonable definition of the writer's range of normal signature variations.[8]

---

[6]Hilton, p. 173.

[7]Osborn, pp. 98–99.

[8]Harrison, p. 298.

Defining the range of normal variation in a sense calibrates the yardstick with which the questioned signatures will be measured. The range of normal variation must be defined *before* the analysis of the signature in question can begin.

In order to make the necessary comparisons of the elements of RHYTHM, it is necessary to begin by copying or photographing the signatures. Each signature is then enlarged from 1.5 to 3 times, and the enlargements are organized on a study board. In making these enlargements, it is important that each signature be enlarged to the same degree. In lieu of photographs, high quality, modern photocopy machines that allow for enlargement of the image can be useful. Good quality, enlarged machine copies can be quickly made and mounted to assemble a satisfactory study board. The examiner must take care that the copies are clear and are not distorted before including them in a study. When it is time to prepare exhibits to illustrate important points during testimony, high quality photographs will be necessary.

In some cases the questioned signature will be of a notably different size than is found in the exemplars. Such variation may result, for example, from the writer's accommodation to the confined area allowed for the signature, or an awkward writing position. In such cases, a second enlargement of the questioned signature should be made, enlarging it to the same overall size as the exemplar material. This print will then be useful in making comparisons of the elements of proportion.

Bringing the enlarged exemplars together on the study board will make it possible to judge the range of normal variation with the unaided eye. Taking each element of proportion in turn, the examiner can make note of the frequency, nature, and scope of the variations.

Through the study of a set of enlarged standards the examiner develops a clear understanding of the subject's normal writing habits and the degree to which each of the individual elements might be expected to vary. These normal variations must be defined *before* any comparison between the exemplars and the signature in question can be made.[9]

When the elemental definitions are finished, they become the yardstick by which the questioned signature will be measured. After the range of normal variations has been defined an enlargement of the questioned signature is added to the study board.[10] When the ele-

[9]Osborn, p. 285.

[10]Hilton, p. 174.

ments of proportion in Q1 are compared with the range of variations defined by the exemplars, any element of comparison which does not match the subject's normal variations will be evident.

Speed, proportion, and pressure are divisible into smaller elements.

Speed

It might seem difficult to explain how one can tell how fast the subject moved the pen, without having been present when the signature was produced. The elements that give indications of writing speed are:

- the presence of small tick strokes,
- the feathering of strokes at the beginning or end of a set of letters,
- the smoothness of any long, curved strokes,
- the smoothness of changes in pressure on the pen.

These elements of speed require further explanation.

Ticks and Feather Strokes

Rapid movement of the pen as it first touches or leaves the surface of the paper results in tick or feathered strokes. Tick strokes are very abrupt, rapidly made, "entry" or "exit" strokes. They are created when the pen is moved sharply onto or away from the paper.

The longer, feathered strokes are produced when writing pressure smoothly increases as the pen is brought to the surface of the paper or smoothly fades as the stroke ends.

Both tick and feather strokes are commonly seen in the signatures of a large proportion of the population.[11] They are a clear example of how a common element in writing can be an important identifier—not because they are an usual feature, but because their presence in a questioned signature indicates that when the signature was produced the pen was moving at a speed too rapid to be controlled by conscious thought.

Smoothness of Curves

The smoothness of any long curves in the subject's signature gives another indication of pen speed. Producing curves at a very slow speed causes an uneven, rough-edged line. As the pen is moved more quickly, the line of a curve becomes more even. As with the tick and feather

---

[11]Osborn, p. 108.

strokes, smooth curved lines in a signature indicate that the pen was being moved at a natural, fairly rapid speed.

A word of caution, it must be noted that the rough line quality associated with slow pen speed may be imperceivable in writings produced with a lead pencil. Pencil writing does not show line quality, hesitation, pen-lifts, pen position, and disconnections as clearly as pen writing.[12]

Smoothness of Changes in Pen Pressure

The degree of pressure put on the writing instrument is indicated by the width and density of the written line. Most writers increase and decrease the pressure on the writing instrument on the upstrokes and downstrokes of their writing. Examination of a collection of known signatures will define where, to what degree and how sharply the subject makes these changes in pressure. The pattern of changes in pen pressure is a very important identifier and will later be discussed as an element of rhythm in its own right.

As an indicator of pen speed, smooth changes in the pressure on the writing instrument are indicative of normal pen speed. A lack of modulation of the pen pressure often causes slowly drawn forgeries to look flat and lifeless when compared to the true signatures of the victim.

The elements of Speed are the first group of elements considered in the comparison process because of the importance of the rhythms of Speed in the detection of false signatures.[13] Many signature imitations are easily identified because they are no more than slowly drawn pictures of the victim's signature. Studied closely, they lack quick entry and exit strokes, show jagged and irregular movements in the long curving strokes and lack normal smoothness in the change of pressure on the pen.

Tracings are the most slowly made imitations and are identified as false signatures by an examination of the elements of Speed. Not only will most tracings show little or no natural pen speed, they often will include pen lifts at odd places such as in the middle of a long curved stroke, hesitation marks, and a general uncertainty of movement.[14]

---

[12]Osborn, p. 332.

[13]Baker, J. Newton. Law of Disputed and Forged Documents. Charlottesville, The Michie Company, 1955, p. 52.

[14]Hilton, p. 187.

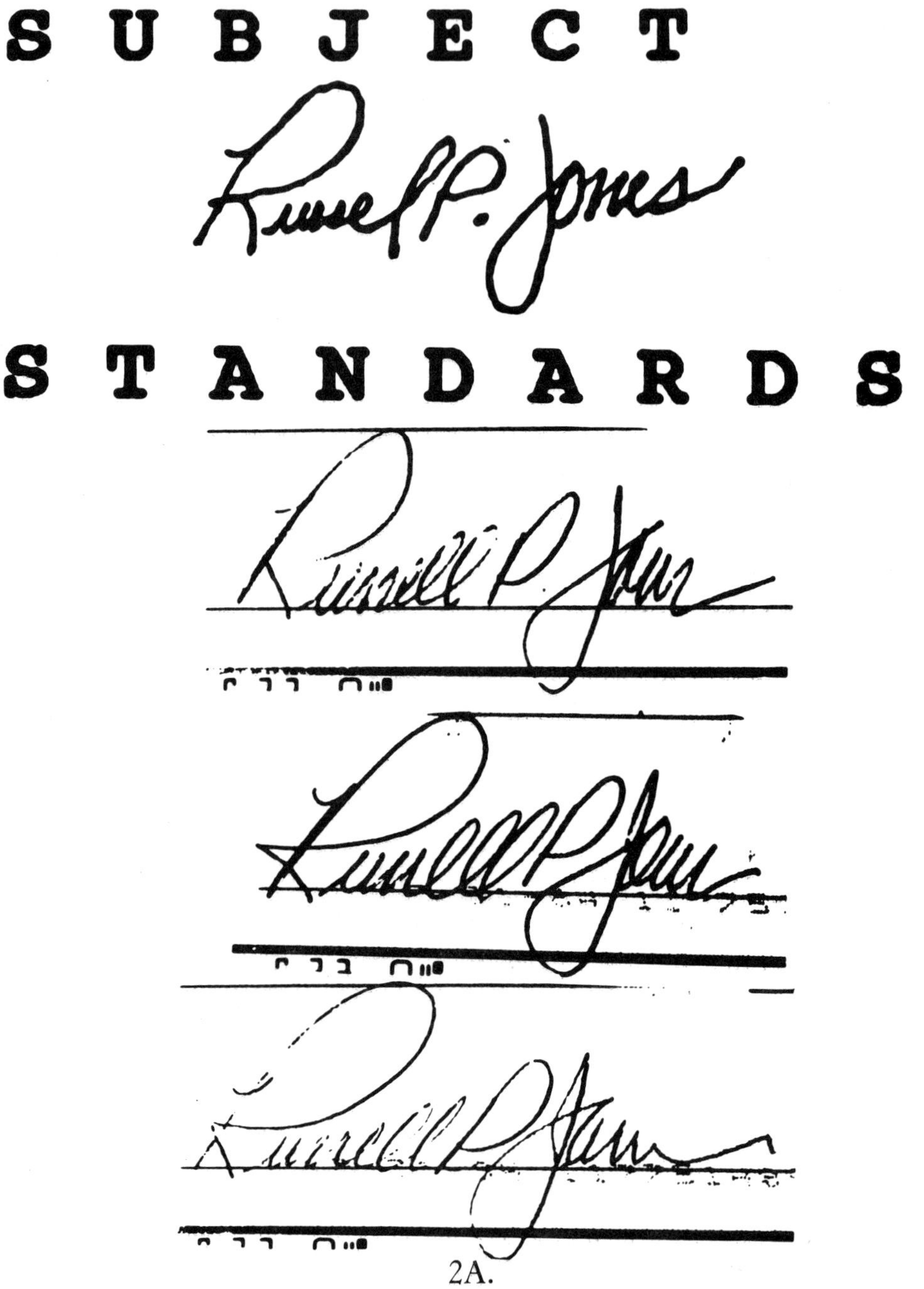

2A.

Illustration 2 A & B. The exemplars for Mr. Jones demonstrate pen speed in the feather strokes at the end of the first name; the smoothness of the large curving strokes in many letters and the smoothness of the changes of pen pressure as shown by the changes in thickness and density of the inked line. The subject signature shows labored, slow pen speed as well as numerous errors in the elements of proportion, pressure and design. (See sample worksheet, Illustration 2B.)

ELEMENTS OF COMPARISON --WORKSHEET

Case ILLUSTRATION #2

Comparison of Q 2 ; SIGNATURE

with the Exemplars for(Set K 1) R. JONES

Ratings: Subject (A;) B; C. Exemplars (A;) B; C.

ELEMENTAL	SECONDARY	PRIMARY	CRITICAL
Ticks & Feather Strokes ≠		(1.) SLOW DRAWING. NO NATURAL FLOW IN THE PEN MOVEMENTS.	
Smoothness of Curves ≠	≠ Speed		
Smoothness of Pressure Changes ≠			
Placement ≠			
Expansion & Spacing ≠			
Top of Writing (TOW) ≠	≠ Proportions	≠ RHYTHMS	
Base of Writing (BOW) ≠			
Angulation/Slant SIMILAR			
Overall Pressure ≠	≠ (1) Pressure		≠ **RHYTHM/FORM BALANCE**
Pressure Change Patterns ≠			
Gross Forms ≠ (2)	(2.) SPELLING ERROR.		
Variations	≠ Design	≠ FORM	
Connective Forms			
Micro-Forms ≠			

REMARKS: Q ≠ K. Q IS A DRAWING OF A SIGNATURE. NO RHYTHM AND ERRORS IN DESIGN.

OPINION/LEVEL OF CERTAINTY: I; II; III; (IV:)

2B.

These pen lifts can be seen by carefully examining the line of the writing using moderate magnification (from 2x to 10x).

Proportions

The elements of Speed examine how fast the writer moves the pen. The elements of proportion examine the direction and distance of each pen movement. It is surprising to see how consistent the rhythms of proportion are found to be when one examines a collection of exemplars.[15] The elements of proportion are:

- Placement of the signature on the preprinted line
- Expansion in and between letters and spacing between names
- The pattern created at the top of writing by the relative height of each letter, as it appears in context. The pattern at the top of the writing compares the height of the middle zone letters and the height of the vertical extension strokes.
- The pattern created at the bottom line of the writing by the relative degree of movement in each descending stroke. The pattern created by the base of each letter and the length of the lower descending strokes are compared.
- Angulation of down-strokes and the slant of the axis of the letters.

Each of these elements must be examined in a representative number of exemplar signatures. The goal is to develop a fair and reasonable definition of the writer's normal variations in the relative sizes, spacings, and angles of the strokes that form the signature. Where a collection of exemplars shows a wide range of variation for an element, a graphic presentation of these variations will be more meaningful than a set of measurement tables.

Placement

Force of habit influences the act of producing a signature even before the pen touches the paper.[16] How the writer uses the available space and places the signature on the preprinted line are decisions made by force of habit. A collection of exemplars will show whether the subject most often places the baseline of the signature on a preprinted line,

[15]Osborn, p. 141.

[16]Harrison, p. 114.

keeps it above the line, allows it to drop below the line, or produces a baseline that rises and falls in a rhythmic pattern.

The examiner will also be able to determine where the subject first brings the pen into contact with the paper and whether the subject starts with the pen already in motion (shown by tick or feather strokes which were examined as elements of Speed) or rests it on the paper before the first stroke.

Expansion and Spacing

There are several elements of proportion which relate to the size of the signature—and more importantly, to the relative sizes of it components. It is not uncommon for a false signature to be of a generally correct, overall size. However, a closer, more detailed analysis of the relationship of each pen movement within the signature often shows that the writer failed to maintain correct proportion of movement from one stroke to the next.

Careful study of most signatures will reveal a habitual relationship between the width of each letter and the space allowed between letters. Like the other elements which combine to make signatures useful for identification, expansion and spacing are the product of habit. Review of the exemplars displayed on the study board will show an individualized pattern in the expansion and spacing of the letters.

As with pen strokes, blank spaces are a part of the signature. Spaces such as those left between the first name, middle initial and last name, spaces after pen lifts, or spaces after capitals, all flow from habit.

As with all of the elements of comparison, exemplars define the subject's habits of pen lifts and spaces left between pen movements. For many writers, this element might show a greater range of variation than other elements. Space left open between sets of pen movements can be affected by the need to fit a signature into a cramped writing space. This rhythm is more often affected by a limited writing area than other elements of comparison.[17]

Top of Writing Pattern

The vertical dimensions of writing are broken down into three zones. The middle zone is the area along the baseline of a signature which is defined by the height of the noncapitalized, or lower case letters com-

---

[17]Osborn, p. 139.

pleted within that zone. Middle zone letters would include the vowels a, e, i, o, u and consonants such as m, n, and c—letters that do not have ascending or descending strokes.

A collection of standard signatures will show a habitual pattern in the relative height of the upstrokes in the middle zone characters. The height of any letter may vary depending on the letter which comes before or after and/or where the letter is used in the name. For example an *m* in the middle of a name might be of a different height than an *m* at the end of the name. With a pattern of such variations defined by a reliable set of exemplars, these habitual idiosyncrasies become useful identifiers.

Study of a collection of exemplars will also show a habitual pattern in the degree of upward movement when the writer produces the extension strokes that form the upper zone of letters such as l, t, b, d, and f. Here again, the height of these extension strokes will often vary with the particular letter being written and with the placement of that letter. I have found, for example, that it is common for many writers to make the letter *t* when it is used in a *th* combination shorter than the *t* at the end of a word or when it preceeds a middle zone letter.

The middle-zone and upper-zone pattern of vertical movements in a signature can be seen by marking the stop point of all vertical pen movements on an overlay. Marking the top-of-writing points of a few of the exemplar signatures will show the pattern and the variations in these pen movements.[18] This graphic chart can be a useful visual aid in presenting the examiner's findings to the court.

Base of Writing Pattern

Descending strokes are the strokes in which the pen is moving down to, or past, the baseline of the writing. Descending strokes in the middle-zone letters form a pattern along the baseline of the signature. For some writers this baseline will be nearly even or straight. For others the descending strokes will form a baseline that rises or falls as the signature is finished.

The descending extensions of the f, g, j, p, q, y, and z are formed in the lower zone of writing. The extent to which these descending strokes move away from the baseline of the writing is, again, determined by habit.

---

[18]Harrison, pp. 312–314.

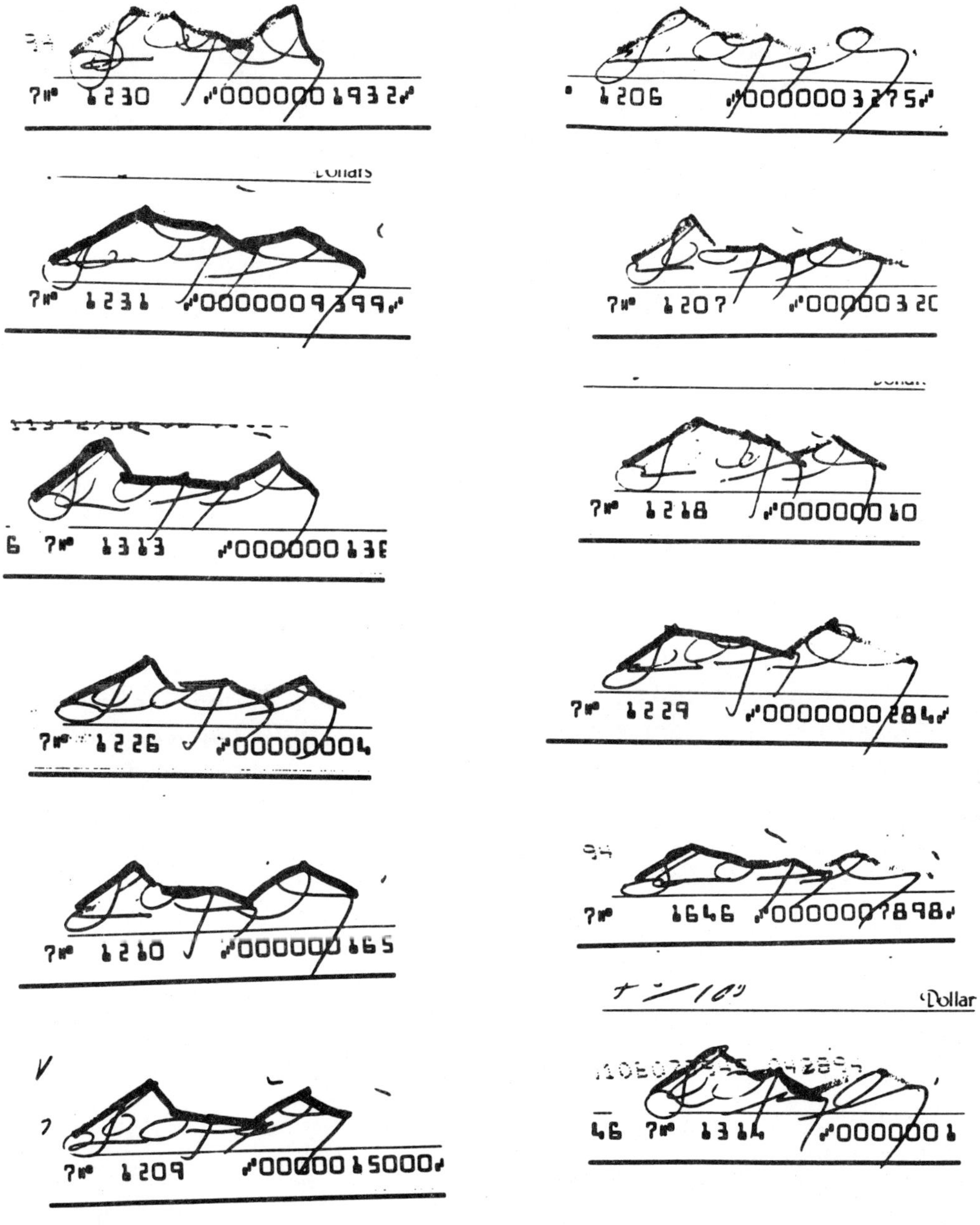

Illustration 3. A copy of the signatures from illustration number one with the top-of-writing pattern marked.

The points at which downward movement of the pen is terminated can be graphically marked on an overlay just as was described for the top-of-writing test. The stopping points along the baseline and the stopping points of any lower extension strokes will form a pattern that is roughly repeated (with natural variations) through a collection of exemplars. As for all of these sets of pen movements, the possible combinations are limitless. What is important to the examiner is to find the habitual rhythmic habit so that it may be used as an identifier. It is common for a forged signature to fail to equal these complex patterns.

Angulation and Slant

The degree of movement in pen strokes is determined by habit; so is the angle at which the pen is moved. The angle of the upstrokes determines the axis or slant of the letter. Writing is said to exhibit a forward slant when the upstrokes are slanted approximately twenty degrees or more, to the right of vertical. Very few writers produce a true backslant with the upstrokes slanted to the left of vertical. Many writings in which the upstrokes are made almost perpendicular to the baseline appear to have a backslant because of the angle of the downstrokes.

Pen movement to the right is most often found in the upstrokes and in the horizontal movements between and within the letters. In forward slanted writings the downstrokes are generally vertical or angled to the left. In some, so-called backslant writings more of the forward movement is accomplished in downstrokes.

The patterns of slant and angulation flow from habit. In many signatures one letter may slant more to the right (or left) than others. While the general slant of a signature might be common, the pattern of variations in slant in the upstrokes and variations in the angulation in the downstrokes becomes quite complex and difficult to successfully imitate.

Pressure

The degree of pressure placed on the pen and the modulation of that pressure are unconscious writing habits. Some writers put only a slight pressure on the writing instrument. Others push on the writing instrument until they nearly destroy the paper. Correctly imitating pen pressure presents a difficult task.

Pressure Modulation

To imitate pressure modulation would require imitating the slightest possible movement at the tip of the pen—a movement too fine to be consciously controlled.

Pressure, and especially the modulation of pressure, are among the most difficult writing habits to successfully imitate.[19] As pressure on the pen changes it creates subtle changes in the density and width of the pen line. Many forgeries appear flat and lifeless because they lack the natural modulation of pen pressure found in the victim's true signatures. (See the subject signature in Illustration 2.)

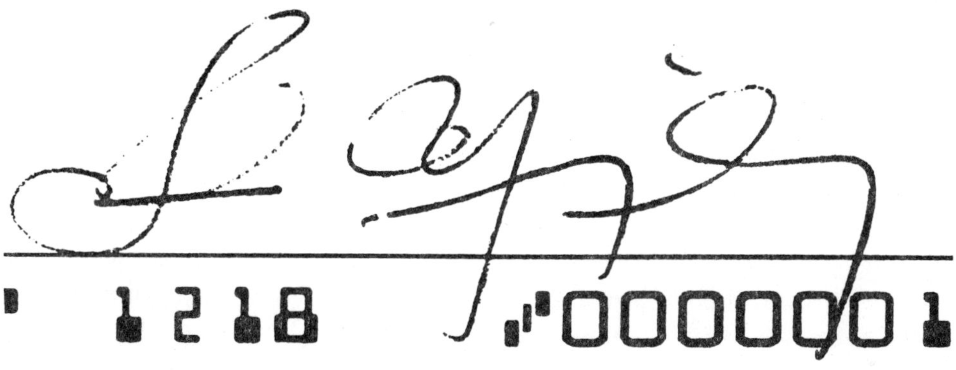

Illustration 4. Modulation of the pressure placed on the pen can be seen in the changes of width and density in the written line. The pattern of these changes can be seen in the signatures on the study board in illustration number one. A pattern of subtle changes in pen pressure is impossible to imitate.

Form

The form used for the letters appearing in a signature may well differ from the form used for the same letters in another word. Signatures represent a graphic design composed of sets of letters and movements. Each set of letters or movements which is separated by a pen lift is referred to as a graphic set. The longer the graphic set, the more important force of habit becomes in producing them rhythmically. Form is examined by making comparisons of the following elements:

- gross forms—the designs used for letters, or sets of letters, made in

[19]Osborn, p. 101.

one graphic set. The longer the graphic set, the more complex the set of habitual movements required to produce it.

• connective forms—the designs created by the strokes that join one letter to the next.

• variations—different designs used for the same letter. Variations of design often are seen when one letter is used in different places within a signature.

• micro-forms—the most subtle aspects of pen handling, such as the interweaving of strokes or nearly invisible pen lifts. These tiny details are usually not visible without magnification.

Detailed analysis and comparison of the designs in the exemplar signatures are easier when the enlargements are displayed on a study board. As in the analysis of the elements of rhythm, the examiner must study sufficient exemplar materials to be satisfied with the fairness and accuracy of the definition of normal variation. The normal variations in the design of the signature must be understood before the questioned signature is brought into the comparison.

The examiner can use photographs or high quality copies to define the variations in design for each letter and each graphic set. The variations themselves are habitual and are significant identifiers.[20] The designs formed by the strokes which join one letter to the next are sometimes as useful for identification as are the letters themselves. Where a signature includes the use of a letter in different placements—for example; an e in the middle of the name and also at the end—any variation in how the letter is formed should be noted.[21]

For the last element of comparison, micro-forms, using a moderate power (6X to 10X) magnifier, the examiner should follow the line of writing and observe the finest details of how the writing instrument is moved and turned in the writer's hand. For example, details of which way the small loops in the top of an *a* are turned should be noted. Where a writing shows some unusual tiny detail it should be recorded in close-up photographs. These tiny, unnoticeable twists and turns are of great importance in the examination.[22]

No one is fully aware of the smallest details included in their signature. Micro-forms are critical to the examiner's decision about a questioned

---

[20]Osborn, p. 208.

[21]Conway, James V.P. Evidential Documents. Springfield, Charles C Thomas, 1978, pp. 48–49.

[22]Osborn, p. 256.

signature. The matching of micro-forms in a questioned signature with the micro-forms defined by the exemplars is strong evidence of common authorship.[23] How else, other than by force of habit, would anyone equal a writing speed too fast to be regulated by conscious thought—and at the same time, produce all of the tiny, nearly invisible, details correctly?

Just to accomplish a successful imitation of the rhythms of a signature requires moving the pen quickly, smoothly, in the correct directions, for the correct distances, with the correct pen pressure, while changing the pen pressure to the correct degree at just the right time. All of this must be done while also producing all of the correct designs right down to the finest detail! Certainly not an easy task.[24, 25]

---

[23]Harrison, p. 419.

[24]Hilton, pp. 185–186.

[25]Osborn, p. 244.

Chapter Four

RECOGNITION OF FALSE SIGNATURES

As habits of pen movement and design become ingrained through years of usage, each person's signature comes to represent a unique balance of the rhythms of pen movement and the designs of the signature's forms. Producing a signature is not a mechanical, unerring act, but rather a dynamic activity which is subject to many influences. In a collection of any person's signatures the balance of rhythm/form will vary. The examiner must study enough exemplar signatures to develop a fair and reasonable definition of the subject's range of normal variations.

Signatures can be said to match when the BALANCE of RHYTHM and FORM in the questioned signature is within the range of normal variation as defined by the exemplars—with an absence of any significant, inexplicable difference.

The forger's challenge is somehow to produce the intricate sets of forms of the true signature, while at the same time correctly producing all of the subtleties of rhythm. Some signatures present the forger with a far more difficult challenge than that posed by other signatures. The degree of skill required of the forger depends on the complexity of the victim's signature and the extent to which the victim's true signatures vary.

There are two general classes of forgery—tracing and simulation. The first class of forgeries are accomplished by *tracing* a genuine signature. Tracing might be accomplished using any of several methods. Despite the method used, the traced signature will show nearly correct forms, but will lack the rhythm and flow of pen movement seen in the true signatures. Errors in matching the elements of Speed are indications of tracing. In many crude tracings, it will be obvious that the pen was lifted in odd places, so that the forger could see the pattern of the true signature before executing the next movement. Retouching or patching of the forms, is common in tracings.

Even though it may be evident the subject signature is a poor quality, retouched drawing that does not match the exemplars, it may not be

Illustration 5A. A crudely traced signature in which an attempt was made to imitate the tremor seen in the standards.

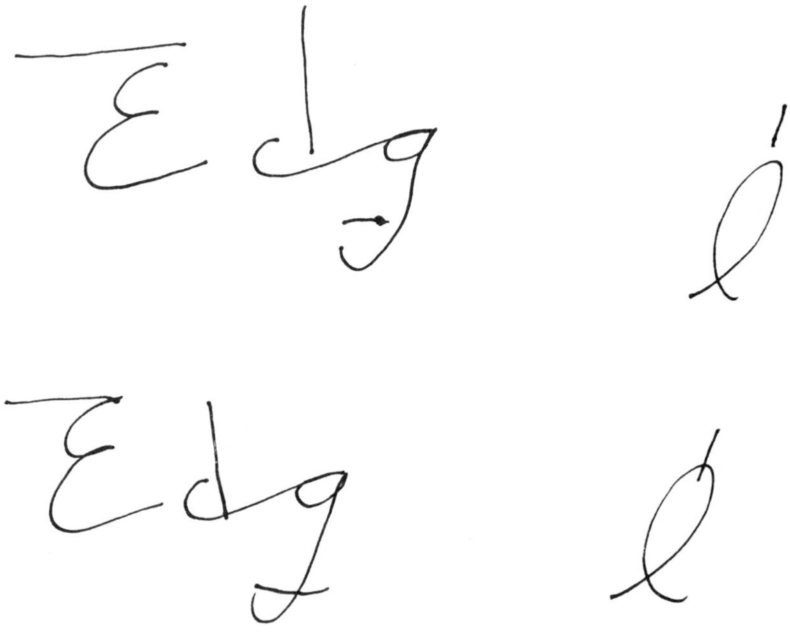

Illustration 5B. A diagram of the strokes used to construct the letters. In the upper sketches the individual strokes are drawn so as to show the pen lifts separating each graphic set. The lower sketch shows how the strokes were assembled. Notice the small stroke added to the top of the letter *l* to imitate the subject's tremor.

possible to determine how it was produced. Without the model signature it may be impossible to determine whether the forgery was prepared by a tracing technique or drawn "freehand." Both types of forgery fail to show natural pen speed.

It is often said that if two signatures match exactly, then one of them must be a traced forgery of the other. The key question here is what does "exactly" really mean? If exactly is taken to mean that when overlaid the signatures match up very closely, then that statement is false. Writers who sign with a dominant rhythm pattern are capable of producing signatures which are quite close to matching when overlaid.[26] Certainly, the rhythms and forms in some of these signatures do not vary, one from the other, to a degree any greater than the margin of error seen in many tracings. When two signatures are found in which every element matches *exactly,* the examiner must look into the possibility of one, or both, of the documents having been composed on a copy machine.

[26]Baker, p. 187.

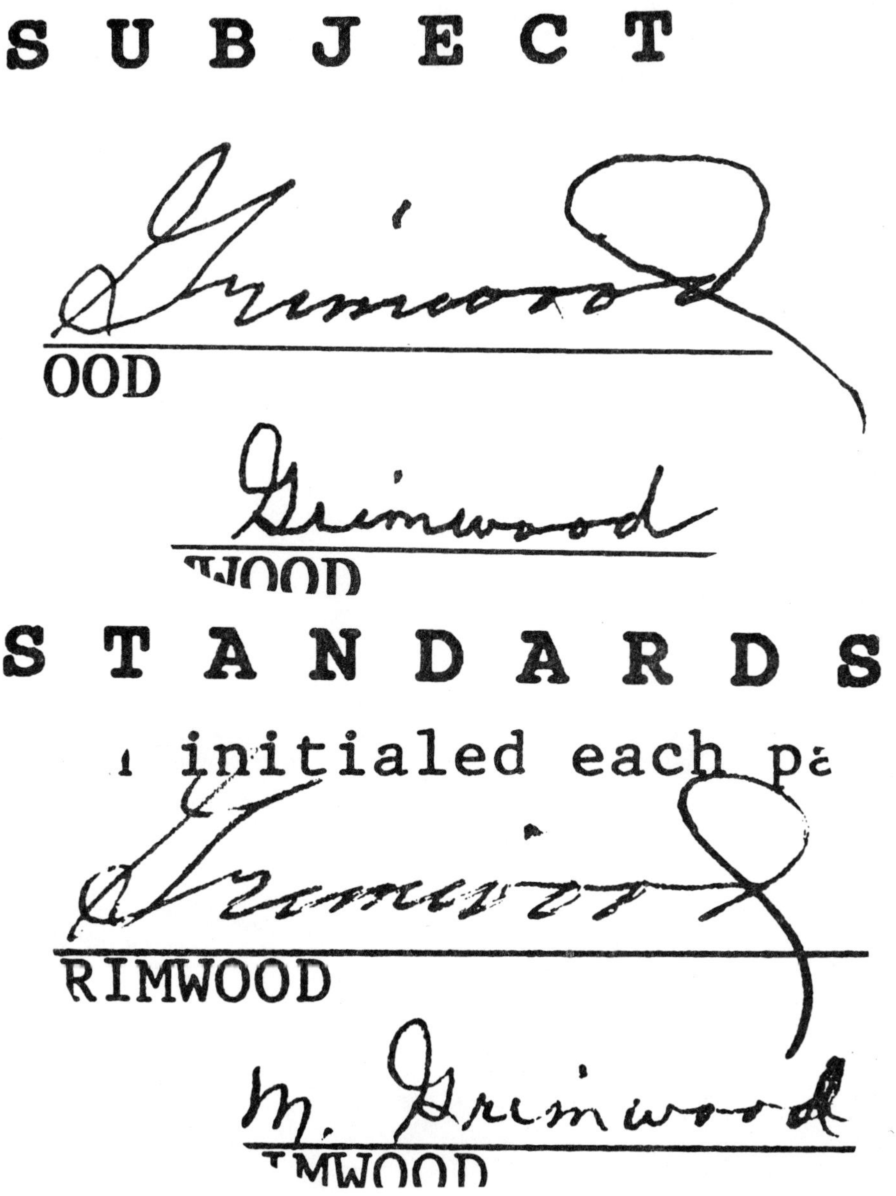

6A.

Illustration 6 A, B & C. Both subject signatures show numerous differences in the elements of rhythm and form when compared with only one exemplar each. (The case was not done as a one-to-one comparison. The materials examined included several exemplars for each name.) Whether these subject signatures were prepared free-hand or by tracing is not known. (See sample worksheets, Illustrations 6B and 6C.) The final *d* in the lower exemplar signature is an example of an accidental flaw in a genuine signature. The writer recognized the flaw and wrote over the letter to correct for it.

ELEMENTS OF COMPARISON --WORKSHEET

Case ILLUSTRATION #6

Comparison of Q 1 ; UPPER MOST SIGNATURE

with the Exemplars for(Set K 1) UPPER MOST EXEMPLAR

Ratings: Subject (A;) B; C. Exemplars (A;) B; C. *CASE INCLUDED NUMEROUS EXEMPLARS

<u>ELEMENTAL</u> <u>SECONDARY</u> <u>PRIMARY</u> **<u>CRITICAL</u>**

(1) SPEED AND PRESSURE ≠ STANDARDS.

PROPORTION AND DESIGN DO = STANDARDS.

POSSIBLE TRACING.

Ticks & Feather Strokes
Smoothness of Curves
Smoothness of Pressure Changes
— ≠ Speed

Placement
Expansion & Spacing
Top of Writing (TOW)
Base of Writing (BOW)
Angulation/Slant
— OK (1) Proportions — ≠ RHYTHMS

Overall Pressure
Pressure Change Patterns
— ≠ Pressure

Gross Forms
Variations
Connective Forms
Micro-Forms
— VERY CLOSE (1) Design — FORM

RHYTHMS + FORM — ≠ **RHYTHM/FORM <u>BALANCE</u>**

REMARKS: Q ≠ K. POSSIBLE TRACING.

OPINION/LEVEL OF CERTAINTY: I; II; III; (IV;)

6B.

ELEMENTS OF COMPARISON --WORKSHEET

Case ILLUSTRATION #6

Comparison of Q 2 ; LOWER SIGNATURE

with the Exemplars for(Set K 2) LOWER EXEMPLAR SIGNATURE

Ratings: Subject (A); B; C. Exemplars (A); B; C. *CASE INCLUDED NUMEROUS EXEMPLARS

ELEMENTAL	SECONDARY	PRIMARY	CRITICAL

(1.) SPEED AND PRESSURE ≠ STANDARDS.

PROPORTIONS AND DESIGN ARE OK (2)

POSSIBLE TRACING

Ticks & Feather Strokes
Smoothness of Curves
Smoothness of Pressure Changes
— ≠ Speed

Placement
Expansion & Spacing
Top of Writing (TOW)
Base of Writing (BOW)
Angulation/Slant
— OK (1) Proportions — RHYTHMS

Overall Pressure
Pressure Change Patterns
— ≠ Pressure

RHYTHM/FORM BALANCE
(2) DIFFERENCES IN imwoo v. im woo

Gross Forms
Variations
Connective Forms ≠ (2)
Micro-Forms ≠ (2)(3)
— VERY CLOSE (1)(3) Design — FORM
(3) DETAILS IN TURN OF PEN AT TOP OF CIRCLE LETTERS.

REMARKS: Q ≠ K. POSSIBLE TRACING.

OPINION/LEVEL OF CERTAINTY: I; II; III; (IV:)

6C.

For rhythmic signatures, tracing or attempted simulation of forms is detected by the relative lack of speed and flow in the questioned signature, and not by the fact that the questioned signature closely matches some other example.[27] Under even moderate magnification, a tracing looks like a poor drawing of the true signature—which is just what it is.

Illustration 7. This is an example of a filled tracing. The signature was first traced with a light line, then a darker pen was used to go over the light line tracing. Where the second tracing was inaccurate the lighter line can be seen in several places. This is a crude method of producing a forged signature.

If the victim's exemplars show a poor writing skill so that the defined normal range of variation includes irregular pen speed, lifts, and even retouchings, then detecting a tracing becomes more difficult. Even in these cases, the examiner should not jump to the conclusion that a questioned signature is traced only because it nearly fits some other example. A close inspection of the micro-forms of the exemplars and the questioned signature will probably resolve the question. In poor attempts, traced signatures may include retouching strokes added to extend a character or stroke to better fit the model. These strokes are apparent when the signature is examined under the microscope. They are a strong indication that the subject signature was traced.

For some elderly or ill persons—writers with diminished writing skills—a traced signature might even show a smoother, better controlled pen handling than is seen in the exemplars. Writer's who have developed a tremor may be seen as easy victims because the forger believes the tremor will mask the indicators of forgery. Genuine tremor is as difficult to imitate as genuine writing movements. The examiner working on such a case will need to examine an extensive collection of exemplars in order to define the patterns and variations in the victim's tremor.[28]

[27]Osborn, p. 344.

[28]Hilton, p. 185.

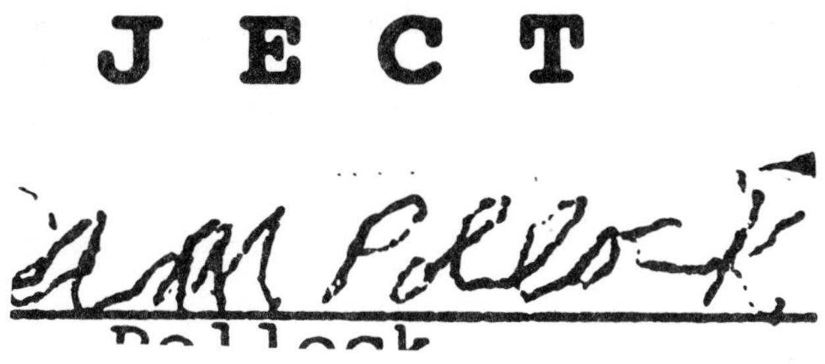

8A.

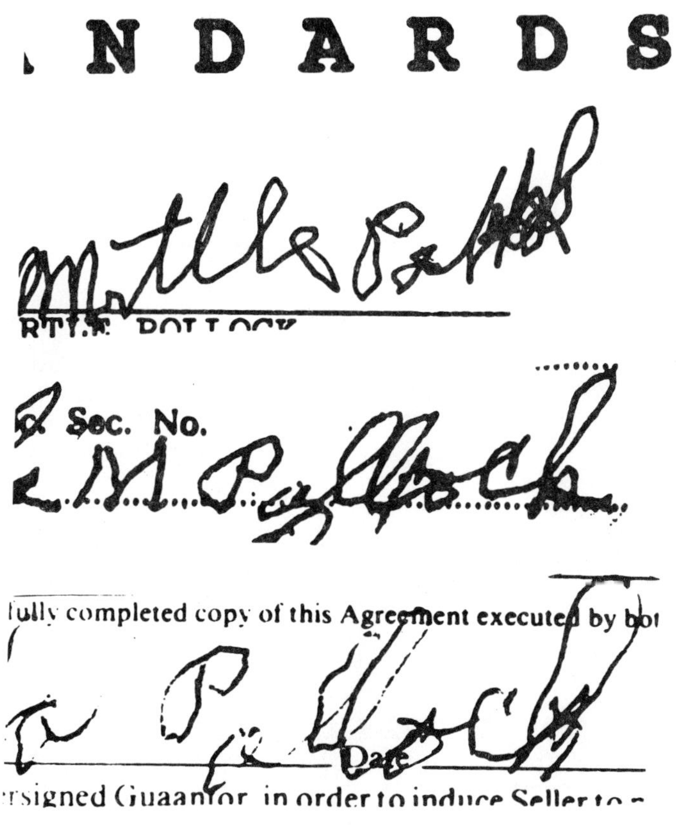

8B.

Illustration 8A, B & C. This subject signature (8A) displays errors of rhythm in the top-of-writing pattern, the base-of-writing pattern, and errors of design. Examination of the micro-forms revealed pen lifts in several places. (See sample worksheet, Illustration 8C.) Compare the nature of the tremor in the subject signature with that in the exemplars (8B). The exemplars show the pen was moved in short straight strokes that angle their way around a curve. The subject signature was perhaps written on a course surface or the pen was shaken while the letters drawn.

ELEMENTS OF COMPARISON --WORKSHEET

Case ILLUSTRATION #8

Comparison of Q 8-A ; SIGNATURE

with the Exemplars for(Set K 1) ILLUSTRATION 8-B, POLLOCK

Ratings: Subject (A;) B; C. Exemplars (A;) B; C.

ELEMENTAL	SECONDARY	PRIMARY	CRITICAL
		(1.) DIFFERENT TYPE OF TREMOR PATTERN.	
Ticks & Feather Strokes			
Smoothness of Curves ≠ (1)	≠ Speed		
Smoothness of Pressure Changes ≠ (1)			
Placement ≠			
Expansion & Spacing ≠			
Top of Writing (TOW) ≠	≠ Proportions	RHYTHMS	
Base of Writing (BOW)			
Angulation/Slant			
Overall Pressure	(1) Pressure		
Pressure Change Patterns			≠ **RHYTHM/FORM BALANCE**
Gross Forms ≠ (2)	(2.) DIFFERENT K		
Variations	≠ Design	FORM	
Connective Forms ≠ (3) LIFTS			
Micro-Forms ≠ (3)			

REMARKS: Q ≠ K. DIFFERENT SPEED; PROPORTION; PRESSURE AND DESIGN.

OPINION/LEVEL OF CERTAINTY: I; II; III; (IV:)

8C.

The second class of forgeries are *simulations,* or *free hand simulations.* There are three types of free hand simulations, those for which the writer tried to imitate the victim's writing rhythms; those for which the focus was on the design of the forms in a victim's signature; and the "simple forgery" in which no attempt is made to imitate the victim's true signature.

Simple forgeries are seen in cases in which the forger did not have a model signature, or chose to ignore a model, and could only write the victim's name. There is no attempt to match the victim's writing habits. The forger writes the victim's name at a natural speed, usually trying to contrive a disguised style and perhaps adding some flourishes to the capitals.

The term simple forgery is a little misleading. An examiner needs to conduct a comparison of the signatures that are claimed to be forged and the victim's exemplars before accepting the statement that the documents in question are actually forged. A common situation arises in which a person uses a new credit card (for example) and signs a contrived signature on the purchase slips. Later they deny the contrived signatures and claim the card was never received. The examiner must address this possibility. Separating a disguised signature by the cardholder from the actual writings of some other person may not be simple at all. Contrived or disguised signatures will be discussed in more detail in Chapter Seven.

In cases where the forger does attempt to imitate a model signature, and the forgery must be produced in public—as is the case when endorsing a stolen check or using a stolen credit card—the writer of a simulated forgery usually attempts to produce the rhythm or flow of the genuine signature. The false signature will include errors of rhythm and will most often display forms not found in the normal variations of the victim's true signature.

In most simulated signatures, the forger is satisfied to capture the general appearance, or pictorial effect, of the genuine signature. In such an attempt, greater attention is given to the appearance of capitals and any flourishes in the signature rather than to the intricacies of the minor forms.

Simulated signatures in which the forger placed emphasis on the design of the characters lack natural pen speed. Such signatures show many of the same characteristics seen in tracings and are described with many of the same adjectives—drawn, built up, artificial, or unnatural. Without access to the model signature it may be impossible to determine whether a poor quality forgery was produced by tracing, or slowly drawn as a free-hand simulation[29] (see Illustration No. 6).

Not all signatures are difficult to simulate. If the intended victim has a very brief and simple signature or one that varies greatly, the forger is presented with an easier task than if the would-be victim's signatures consistently included rhythmic, complex movements. There are three types of signatures which present even a moderately skilled forger with a relatively easy task. For each type, it is unlikely that any document examiner would be able to identify a skilled forgery.

Some writers put great emphasis on only one-half of the rhythm/form balance. Whether the emphasis is on rhythm or on forms, the lack of a complex balance of the two makes the forger's task easier.

This signature, for instance, shows an overemphasis on the elements of rhythm, especially speed.

Illustration 9. A signature which is produced with fast rhythmic pen movements but with no complex forms. Lacks rhythm/form balance.

The pen is moved quickly, but there is no complexity to the movement. An imitator can simulate this rapid movement with little danger of making a detectable error. Using a quickly written slurred set of pen strokes as a signature makes a forger's task easy work.[30] Many who produce such a careless signature also have a wide range of normal variations in their signatures. That wide range of variations makes the forger's task even easier!

On the other hand, in this example the pen is moved carefully to make forms with slow, deliberate movements and very little individualized rhythm.

In this case an imitator could work just as slowly and exactly as does the subject.

Simulating either very fast, indistinct movements or simple, slow

---

[29]Osborn, pp. 326–329.

[30]Harrison, p. 310.

Illustration 10. A signature which is produced with slow, uniform pen movements but with no complex integration of rhythms. Also lacking rhythm/form balance.

movements does not present the forger with a difficult task. Forgery is detectable when the forger makes an error of rhythm or form, which causes the forged signature to differ significantly from the range of normal variation defined by the exemplars. Writers whose natural signatures are at one extreme or the other make it easier for the forger to stay within the range of normal variations—and they become easy victims for a forger.[31]

The third class of writers who are easy prey for forgers are those who are so careless or so unskilled, that a collection of their true signatures shows each one to vary from the others. Writers whose signatures vary greatly, present the forger with a "target" so large that it takes in virtually any probable errors. The forger's "errors" of rhythm or form will very likely present the examiner with no variations of rhythm or form not also seen in the exemplars.

If the forger's target is either very large—with a wide range of variation in a simple name—or very easy to hit—extreme emphasis on rhythm or extreme emphasis on form, without complex balance of rhythm and form—even the most skilled document examiner will find it impossible to separate the real from the spurious.

While it is true that some forgers move the pen slowly, resulting in little more than a drawing of the true signature, while other forgeries show the normal pen speed and flow of natural handwriting. A special class of forgery exists when a family member or employee is used to signing, and comfortable with signing, another person's name. Some secretaries frequently sign for their bosses; or spouses sign for one another. If the genuine signature in such a case presents a unique rhythm/form balance, the examiner can expect to find *numerous* elemental differences in the imitations, despite the forger's familiarity with the victim's signature. Even in cases when the suspected forger is very familiar with the signature, and comfortable with the act of signing the

[31]Osborn, p. 100.

other person's name, a questioned signature that displays only an isolated, elemental difference is most probably a genuine signature.

A special note of caution is due here. When an examiner is aware of a situation in which a secretary, or a spouse, routinely signs for someone else, great care is necessary to secure reliable standards. The examiner is very apt to err if the secretary's routine imitations are incorrectly accepted as variations in the habits of the subject.

Some forgers cannot resist the temptation to retouch and try to repair obvious errors in form. The most skillful will know that such patching only serves to draw more attention to the flaws.

With the above limitations acknowledged, it must be said that, by far, most signatures are sufficiently complex to thwart successful forgery, and almost all forgeries can be detected through systematic work by an experienced expert. However, having detected the forgery, one is still a long way from finding the forger.

Chapter Five

MATERIALS FOR COMPARISON

Exemplars

Exemplars are the known or self-acknowledged, true signatures of any person. Examination of a questioned signature begins with a detailed study of the exemplar materials. The terms exemplars and standards for comparison, or standards, are often used interchangeably. A collection of anyone's signatures will show that each element of rhythm and form varies slightly. For example, some letters may show slight differences of slant or form from one signature to the next. The extent of these variations is minor for some writers and quite extensive for others.

"How much exemplar writing is enough?" is a question that must be answered for each individual writer in the context of each case. Some writers will show little variation, even between their most careful and most careless signatures. For such subjects relatively few exemplars may satisfactorily define their range of normal variation. The signatures of other writers will vary greatly. The more variation found as the exemplars are gathered, the greater will be the need for an extensive collection of exemplar materials.

The object is to gather writings until the collected materials provide the basis for a fair and reasonable definition of the subject's signature habits and range of normal variation. No specific, minimum number of exemplars can be expressed.

An examiner might begin to compare Q1 with as few as four or five exemplars. More exemplars will be needed but, as a practical matter, when comparing a questioned signature with the exemplars of the victim, once the range of normal variation defined by the collected exemplars includes the variations seen in the questioned signature, then obviously, there is no need to search for further exemplars. For nearly all writers, twelve to twenty exemplars will produce a reasonably complete definition of normal variations.

There are two types of exemplar signatures. NCB exemplars are documents signed by the subject in the normal course of business. Some authors refer to these as collected exemplars. Request exemplars are writings and signatures produced by the subject only to provide the examiner with materials for an examination.

Ideally, at least some of the NCB exemplars will have been produced around the same time as the writing in question. Canceled checks, mortgages or deeds, business papers, receipts, voter registration or poll records, public licenses, hospital permits, letters, greeting cards, and so forth, are frequently the sources for normal-course-of-business exemplars.

Most writers have three and sometimes four styles of writing.[32] The four styles can be easily remembered as the four "C's." The first three are: *C*areful, *C*ommon, and *C*areless. The fourth "C" is *C*ontrived writing. Contrived or disguised writing will be discussed later.

The careful, or formal style, is generally used in the most important writings, or when legibility is stressed. Careful writing may also be seen when some unusual writing circumstance causes the subject to slow down and write with conscious attention to the movements of the pen. For some subjects, the care taken when signing may change depending on the importance placed on the document being signed. For example, a will or a contract might show a more carefully done signature than the subject normally exhibits on a check or a personal note.

The common, or everyday, signature style is more rapidly produced than is careful writing. Exemplars of common signatures are found on canceled checks, personal notes and letters and routine business writings.

Careless writing is done quickly and is often illegible even to the writer. Signatures on credit card or gasoline receipts and the writing of notes taken while on the telephone are possible sources of careless writings.

NCB exemplars are the preferred class of exemplar materials. NCB material can be more difficult to collect than request exemplars, but it is worth the time and effort to secure exemplars free from disguise and distortion.[33] A set of exemplars gathered from NCB materials should include examples from each of the three style levels. Documents of similar significance, produced close to the same time as the questioned signatures are the most valuable exemplars.

---

[32]Conway, p. 12.

[33]Baker, p. 78.

Working with NCB materials does require that the examiner take added precautions. It is important to make certain that each signature accepted into a collection of NCB exemplars can be proven to be the subject's true signature. It is common for spouses to sign some types of documents for one another. Pay check endorsements or greeting cards might be routinely signed by a spouse. In some offices it is common practice for secretaries to sign a manager's name on routine letters. Great care must be used in accepting signatures as exemplars.

Any signature that cannot be clearly supported as an example of the subject's true signature should not be used. When the exemplar set is assembled on a study board, the exemplars should be reviewed as a set. Any signature that exhibits unusual variations should be double checked to be certain that it is from a reliable source. Unless the examiner personally witnesses the subject producing signatures or writings, any materials accepted for use as exemplars can only be viewed as the *purported writing* of that individual. The most publicized mistakes made by competent examiners have resulted from the examiner's acceptance of tainted writings as genuine exemplars.

When sufficient NCB exemplars cannot be collected, the alternative is to have the subject produce request exemplars. Whether consciously or unconsciously, request exemplars are likely to be carefully written. Knowing that the materials are going to be carefully analyzed, it is common for people to experience some difficulty when trying to produce request exemplars that show natural, relaxed writing.

The subject producing request exemplars should be asked to produce each of the three style levels—careful, common, and careless writings. Request exemplars should be taken in sufficient volume, and over a long enough period of time, that a full measure of the subject's writing habits and variations is displayed in the materials produced. It is reasonable to expect that taking a full collection of request exemplars will require an hour or two of work with the typical subject. Explaining what will be needed and how much time the session will require makes it easier to get cooperation and thus results in a more natural set of writings.

To assess the naturalness of the request writings, it is valuable for the examiner to have at least one example of NCB materials with which to verify that the request signatures are not contrived.[34] Even though the analysis may be focused on signature comparison, interrupting the

---

[34]Hilton, p. 321.

production of signatures to have the subject produce written text material and sign other persons' names will help assure that the request signatures are examples of the subject's usual writing habits. If, based on some NCB materials or watching the subject write, the examiner does not believe the request writings represent the subject's natural writing habits, it may become necessary to repeat the session after a few days have passed.

As the analysis proceeds, the examiner will be weighing the significance of any differences between the writing habits defined by the exemplar set and the signatures in question. The exemplars—whether normal course of business materials, request materials, or a combination of both—must be sufficient to give the examiner a fair and reasonable definition of the writing habits of the subject. Until normal variations have been defined, it is not possible to know the significance of the writing habits shown in the questioned materials.

Document examiners are sometimes asked to make a comparison between a questioned signature and a single exemplar signature. Obviously, a single exemplar signature cannot define the subject's range of normal variation. With a great deal of experience, and only after the concept of rhythm/form balance is fully understood, it will sometimes be possible to make a reliable one-to-one comparison of signatures. When the questioned and exemplar signature can be seen to have equal and individualized rhythms and forms, including micro-forms, the experienced examiner might be comfortable expressing an opinion based on a single exemplar.

The decision as to when a one-to-one comparison can be reliably done requires a great deal of experience. The examiner pressed to make a one-to-one comparison is generally wise to decline the work until sufficient material can be gathered. For any examiner, regardless of depth of experience, an opinion based on a one-to-one comparison is set on a weak foundation if it is to be defended against a rigorous cross-examination.

The matching of individualized rhythm/form balance with the presence of matching micro-forms can support an opinion that the two signatures are from the same source. However, it is not reasonable practice to try to support an opinion that a signature is not genuine based only on a one-to-one comparison. Differences, even gross differences, cannot be given proper consideration until the subject's range of variation has been defined.

Copybook Writings

The elements of writing are frequently discussed with the terms "class characteristics" and "individualized characteristics." Class characteristics are those writing habits of character form, size, and style which are so common that they are, by themselves, of limited value in identification. Often class characteristics closely adhere to the writing style taught in school—copybook writing.

Individualized characteristics are just what the term implies, personalized habits of rhythm or design. Individualized characteristics always carry greater evidentiary weight than do class characteristics. As with physical features, in combinations, class characteristics take on individuality.

It is my belief that document examiners need to rethink the notion that every person's writing habits can be, or need be, traced back to the influence of one or another copybook style. Copybook training may well have been important in the United States several decades ago, and it may still be taught with serious discipline in some parts of the world. In today's American school systems, however, few students are greatly influenced by copybook teaching. Most teachers place little emphasis on conforming to copybook style.

Generally, regardless of the copybook style taught in second or third grade, there is little or no follow-through in subsequent grades. Beyond attempting to require legibility, few teachers correct the student who fails to adhere rigidly to correct copybook forms. During adolescence, students often copy one another's writing, designs from a teacher's writing or a parent's writing and, of course, they experiment with styles of their own design.

As a rule of thumb, most writers achieve handwriting maturity in their middle-to-late twenties. The elements of writing rhythm and character design become habitual, and from that time on the individual's signature and writing can be expected to change little for as long as the subject is in good health.[35]

Studying copybooks will not teach the examiner to recognize common writing habits. There is no substitute for experience in learning the critical skills required to recognize characteristics commonly found in handwritings. Attentive observation of hundreds upon hundreds of hand-

---

[35]Baker, p. 47.

writings from different groups of people is the only way to develop a clear sense of the common and unusual in handwriting.

For today's expert, the classification of writing forms as copybook or noncopybook is not meaningful. Writing skills can be better classified as common, inferior to common, or superior to common in terms of the writer's integration of writing rhythms and individuality of character design.

Earlier it was noted that the problems of signature identification are similar to some of the problems encountered in making a physical identification. The fact that a subject is of a common height or of common weight is not, by itself, of great value in a physical identification. The term common means only that a particular measurement falls within a range of heights or weights shared by a large part of the general population. In the same sense, handwriting elements may fall into a range of commonly seen rhythms or forms.

Handwriting represents an integrated balance of the elements of rhythm and design. Each of the elements of handwriting can be rated against an approximate, normal distribution. An element can be considered to be within the broad norm if, in the examiner's experience, that element could be expected to appear often in writings collected from the relevant universe of possible writers. For example, considering writings produced by the general, adult American educated population, the norms for the handwriting elements can be described as follows:

Speed

Occasional feathering of initial or final strokes
Smooth line in curved strokes
Smooth changes in pen pressure

Proportions

Even zone balance
Even letter size in the middle zone
Moderate right slant
Even expansion and moderate spacing between names

Pressure

Moderate pressure on writing instrument
Slight increase in pressure on downstrokes

Form

Recognizable character designs

Few differences in design depending on placement
No unusual, small details of pen-handling

For other groups, such as adolescent girls, the very poorly educated, foreign educated or the elderly, many of these norms would not apply. For example, the habit of making i-dots as daisies with little faces on them was popular with a number of girls in one high school. Such an unusual i-dot could be a valuable identifier in a universe of adult writers. In the universe of adolescent girls, however, it was of less value.

Consideration must be given to the norms for the universe of possible writers in question. It would be highly unlikely that any individual's writing would fall within the most common norms for every element. Identification must be based on combinations of elements—in combinations, even common characteristics become individualized. Considering the endless numbers of possible variations in each writing element, it is probable, given sufficient material with which to work, that every person's writing is sufficiently individualized to allow identification.

Chapter Six

DIFFERENCES

In an ideal case, the examiner would have an unlimited number of NCB materials. From this pool, exemplars could be drawn forth until no signature could be found which showed a variation not already demonstrated in the selected materials. In this ideal case, the examiner could say with complete confidence that the exemplars fully define the range of normal variation in the signature habits of that subject. Against such a fully calibrated yardstick a questioned signature could be tested and almost any variation would be significant.

The ideal case, however, is extremely rare. Most often, the document examiner must handle cases with less than ideal circumstances. Exemplars may be limited, hard to locate, untimely, and, if working with request standards, overcontrolled or contrived. In many cases, after exhaustive work, the examiner is left to make judgments as to the significance or cause of some remaining difference. Difficult problems can arise when an examiner finds differences in a questioned signature and then must weigh the significance of those differences.

An examiner who believes some difference in the questioned signature to be insignificant—or, believes that the cause of a significant difference can be explained—faces additional challenges when it is time to testify. Any good attorney can turn an adjective into an argument. When an examiner's opinion relies on the *insignificance* of clearly noticeable differences—or, the examiner must attempt to *explain the causes* of such differences—that examiner must be well prepared to give convincing support to that opinion.

The document examiner should never try to reach beyond the boundaries of this discipline. If an explanation for differences, such as the writer's health condition, calls for expertise beyond that of the document examiner, then that supporting testimony should be offered by other witnesses as part of the attorney's complete case. In the end, to be acceptable, any explanation for differences must pass the critical test for evidence. It must be demonstrable, and reasonable, to convince the average juror.

Faced with a case in which the examiner believes that differences can be explained, some have been tempted to present patronizing testimony. First, lengthy testimony about the examiner's credentials and experience is given. Then the heart of the expert's opinion is expressed in a tone that implies, "Trust me, I know best." Usually this type of testimony is presented without exhibits and with no intention of explaining the examiner's reasoning to the court.[36] If an expert is allowed to get away with such testimony the fault lies with the attorney responsible for the cross-examination. In no case should an attorney allow an expert to leave the jury with an "I say so" opinion, or an opinion based on the "unexplained mysteries" of the science. When an expert is testifying to an opinion arrived at by some special magic, the opposing attorney should not allow that testimony to be accepted as if it were science.

Significance of Differences

An examiner faces a difficult problem when, after careful examination of all available exemplars, the findings include individualized writing habits that match, as well as some notable difference in the writings compared. Are the differences significant? Can they be dismissed as only minor variations, or should they be given more weight, precisely because they are subtle? Are they the gross differences that can signal attempted disguise, or are they really the writing of a different person? Equally qualified examiners can, and do, reach opposing opinions, after arriving at different answers to these questions.

Some examiners have lived by the simplistic rule that unless signatures match perfectly they cannot be by the same writer. It is dangerous to live by simplistic rules. The danger of this particular oversimplification is that a valid signature which includes some minor variation—or a clearly explainable variation—may be declared a forgery.[37] The document examiner must be qualified to analyze the significance of, and causes of, the small differences found between questioned and exemplar signatures. To make decisions based on a simplistic black-and-white rule

[36]Conway, p. 67.

[37]Harrison, pp. 343–344.

does not fulfill the responsibilities of a document examiner.[38] It does not require expert knowledge or skills to simply observe whether letters in a signature fit together hand-in-glove.

The Elements of Comparison chart identifies writing characteristics at four levels of importance—Elemental, Secondary, Primary, and Critical. The least important are the elemental characteristics. As the elements are brought into more complex secondary characteristics—Speed, Proportions, Pressure, and Design—the evidentiary weight becomes greater. The importance given to any difference found in an examination depends on the level of comparison at which that difference can be identified.

Isolated, elemental differences are generally insignificant. For example, a slight difference in the height or angle of a stroke, a pen lift, or an odd change of pressure which does not effect the overall consideration at the secondary level, can be safely considered to be insignificant. To conclude that a signature is not genuine solely because of an isolated, elemental difference would be absurd.

When an elemental factor varies enough to affect the secondary level of comparison, it becomes quite significant. Examples of such a variation would be: lack of matching smoothness and feathering of strokes sufficient to indicate a different pen speed; a mismatch in the proportions of a signature; or failure to match the way the writer changes a character design when it is used in different places.

When the examiner notes a significant difference, the next consideration becomes whether there exists a legitimate reason for that difference. Perhaps the difference is explainable, even though it is not repeated in any volume of exemplars. Such a situation may occur in attempted disguise, in a signature influenced by health or drug problems, or what Hilton refers to as handwriting accidents.[39] When it is believed there may be a reasonable explanation for a difference, the examiner needs to find out whether there is any support for the explanation.

A thorough search of recognized texts and articles may provide an accepted basis for explaining why the subject signature is different from the standards. Perhaps experts from another field, such as medicine, will be needed to explain the effects of an illness or medication. The basic requirement for an explanation of differences is the same as for other document evidence: that which cannot be illustrated and/or demon-

---

[38]Baker, p. 148.

[39]Hilton, pp. 174–175.

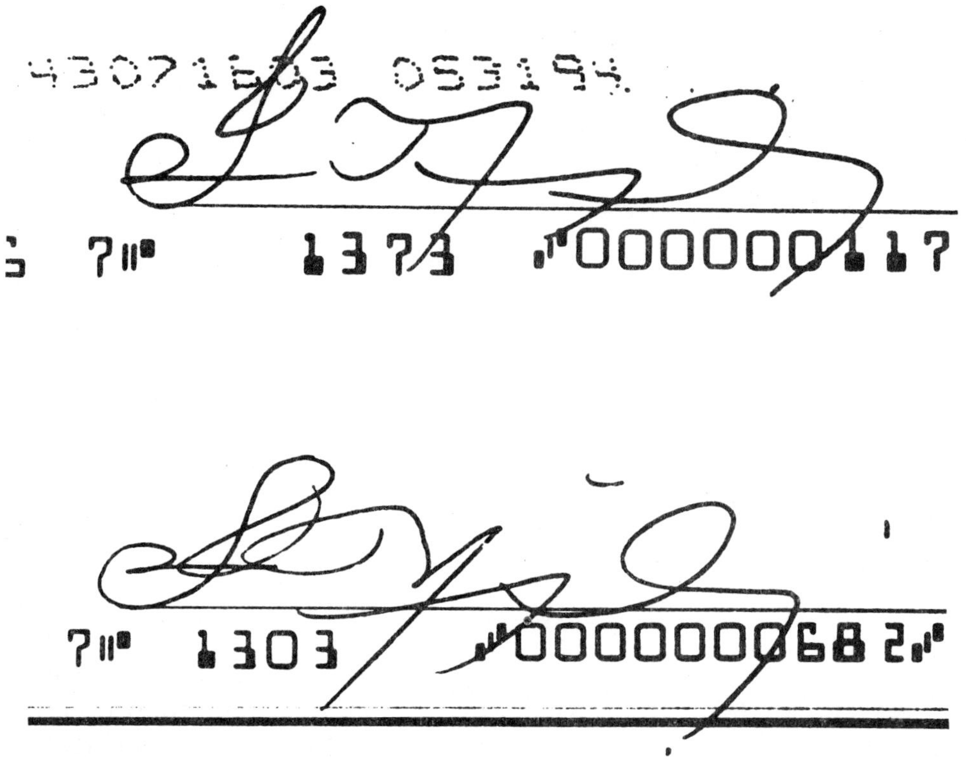

11A.

Illustration 11A, B, C & D. Compared with the study board presented in Illustration 1, the signatures shown here each show an isolated, elemental difference in the second graphic set. A search of more than 200 canceled checks did not produce another example of either of these variations. Neither the pen lift in 11A nor the unusual *v* construction in 11B, affect the overall proportions of the writing. Certainly such elemental differences do not disturb the rhythm/form balance of these signatures. (See sample worksheets, Illustrations 11C and 11D.)

ELEMENTS OF COMPARISON --WORKSHEET

Case ILLUSTRATION #11

Comparison of Q 11-A ; SIGNATURE

with the Exemplars for(Set K 1) STUDY BOARD IN ILLUSTRATION #1

Ratings: Subject (A;) B; C. Exemplars (A;) B; C.

ELEMENTAL	SECONDARY	PRIMARY	CRITICAL
		(1) LIFT IN ONE GRAPHIC SET.	
Ticks & Feather Strokes Smoothness of Curves (1) Smoothness of Pressure Changes	OK Speed		
Placement Expansion & Spacing Top of Writing (TOW) Base of Writing (BOW) Angulation/Slant	OK Proportions	OK RHYTHMS	
Overall Pressure Pressure Change Patterns	OK Pressure		OK **RHYTHM/FORM BALANCE**
Gross Forms Variations Connective Forms Micro-Forms	OK Design	OK FORM	

REMARKS: Q = K. ONE DIFFERENCE -- PEN LIFT IN CAPITAL.

OPINION/LEVEL OF CERTAINTY: (I;) II; III; IV:

11B.

ELEMENTS OF COMPARISON --WORKSHEET

Case ILLUSTRATION #11-B

Comparison of Q 11-B ; SIGNATURE

with the Exemplars for(Set K 1) STUDY BOARD IN ILLUSTRATION #1

Ratings: Subject (A); B; C. Exemplars (A); B; C.

ELEMENTAL	SECONDARY	PRIMARY	CRITICAL
Ticks & Feather Strokes Smoothness of Curves Smoothness of Pressure Changes	OK Speed		
Placement Expansion & Spacing Top of Writing (TOW) Base of Writing (BOW) Angulation/Slant	OK Proportions	OK RHYTHMS	
Overall Pressure Pressure Change Patterns	OK Pressure		OK **RHYTHM/FORM BALANCE**
Gross Forms (1) Variations Connective Forms Micro-Forms	(1) SLIGHT DIFFERENCES IN ONE CAPITAL OK Design	OK FORM	

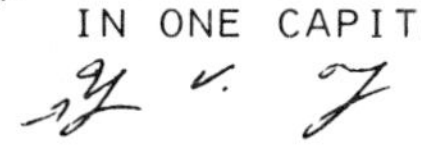

REMARKS: Q = K. ONE DIFFERENCE IN DESIGN OF CAPITAL.

OPINION/LEVEL OF CERTAINTY: (I); II; III; IV:

11C.

strated in a way that would convince the average juror is of very little value.

There are cases in which the question of genuineness of signatures is not answerable. Inconclusive findings are perfectly in order when the examiner is presented with a case that presents only limited rhythm/form balance, or an extremely wide range of normal variations. It would be unusual for two qualified examiners to reach contradictory opinions in such cases. Qualified examiners may contradict each other when signatures show matching, individualized rhythm/form balance, and one of the examiners places too great an importance on an isolated, elemental difference.

Writing, even when signing one's own name, is not a precise, mechanical act. Habit usually guides the movements of a pen within the writer's range of variation, but it does not guarantee that every signature will be flawlessly executed. When some pen movement strays from the writer's usual pattern, habit will cause the writer to correct the error and bring the pen back on track. A slight variation in the proportions of a letter, a difference in spacing or height, even a misplaced pen lift or pressure change in a signature, can be a perfectly normal glitch.

To reach an opinion that a subject signature is not genuine the examiner must find that it shows a significant difference of writing rhythm or form. If an explanation for the differences is offered, the examiner must take that explanation into consideration. Not all significant differences are indicative of forgery. Some comparisons will show significant differences for which there is an understandable cause.

Chapter Seven

EXPLAINING DIFFERENCES

In some cases it is clear to everyone concerned that the questioned signature, or writing, does not match the exemplars. The questioned writing may present significant differences at the secondary, or even the primary, level. However, it is believed that the mismatch is due to some explainable cause. The critical questions for the examiner are: Can these differences be reasonably explained? Are the differences due to an odd writing position, not similarly represented in the exemplar writings? Are they due to illness, or drugs, or drinking? Or, is the explanation being offered only as a means by which to explain away the errors of a forger?[40]

In such cases, an important early step is to take statements from all parties claiming to have knowledge of the circumstances surrounding the production of the signature. These parties might include family members, friends, witnesses, the notary or medical personnel. Their statements should explain in great detail the conditions under which each party believes the writing was produced. Later, the document examiner will attempt to determine whether the physical evidence presented by the documents supports the purported history of production and storage. To verify the testimony explaining differences shown in a signature, it is critical to seek out a large collection of NCB exemplars for the writer in question.

Many factors can cause a signature to include forms, or rhythms, that are not the subject's usual habit. Age, writing position, fatigue, medication, intoxication, illnesses, poor lighting, a faulty writing instrument, an unusual writing surface, depression, emotionalism, or anger are some of the factors that might produce an atypical writing.

If some reoccurring factor is believed to have caused the subject signature to be unusual, the examiner must search for some exemplar writing that most nearly duplicates the circumstances surrounding the

[40]Harrison, p. 345.

signature in question. If the writer was on medication, the examiner must seek other writings produced during a similar course of treatment. Hospital admission records, permits, and release forms, together with doctor's office sign-in sheets and records are possible sources for signatures that relate to the subject's documented state of health and medical history.

Alcohol is frequently cited as the reason for an unusual signature. When it is believed that the writing was produced while the writer was intoxicated, then the examiner must try to find other writings believed to have been produced when the writer was in a similar condition. Credit card receipts signed in bars or restaurants might be especially useful. The object is to locate receipts which can be correlated with the purchase of cocktails.

Sometimes a writer's signature is believed to have been affected because it was penned while in an odd position, such as sitting in a car. When possible, take request exemplars from the subject under duplicated conditions. If request exemplars cannot be taken, then search for other documents that may have been signed under similar circumstances. With the popularity of drive-through banking, "signed while sitting in the car" is frequently the reason for a check signature or endorsement that does not match the exemplars. It may be possible to obtain microfilm records of the subject's other banking transactions conducted at drive-in service windows.

If the circumstances surrounding the production of the writing in question were accidental or transitory, it is unlikely that exemplars produced under similar conditions will be found. Any examination will have to depend on the definition of normal variations developed from available exemplars. The level of certainty of the examiner's opinion will be limited by any elements of rhythm or form shown in the questioned signature which are not included in the limited definition of habits developed from the exemplars. Even with a plausible explanation for differences, the examiner will have to offer an opinion with some limited level of certainty.

Medical Problems

The complex perceptive/motor activities involved in handwriting are sensitive to a great many health problems and medical treatments. From problems as common as a cold or flu to cases of severe brain tumors, health certainly affects our ability to write or sign normally.

The effects of illnesses and drugs on handwriting skills have not been adequately researched. A great deal more well-designed, well-controlled research is needed. The scope and sophistication which research work requires is beyond the resources of private document laboratories, and, in the United States, there is virtually no government money allocated for questioned document research studies.

Some examiners have done a limited amount of quality research into the effects of diseases and treatments on handwriting skills. At least one professional association has consistently tried to advance knowledge in this area. Unwisely, some examiners will offer their own ideas (researched poorly or not at all) as to what to expect with certain medical diagnoses. The effects of medical problems on handwriting skills is an area where some graphologists (those who claim to assess personality based on analysis of handwriting) make extraordinary claims.

Too little is known to lend scientifically sound support to theories about the specific changes in writing skills resulting from illness or drugs. Changes in writing skill due to illness or drugs often are not constant, even for the same patient. A patient who has been unable to sign a form may be able to sit up and write a letter a few hours later.

If timely, normal-course-of-business exemplars can be located, and most health related influences on writing ability can be incorporated into the subject's defined range of normal variation. At least, the developed definition will show whether the changes in question are reasonably seen as further changes in the elements being effected by the illness. Importantly, these exemplars will make inconsistencies in a forged signature easier for the examiner to recognize. It is as difficult for a forger to accurately imitate the victim's declining skills as it would be to imitate the smoother rhythm of earlier signatures (Illustration 8).

When a questioned document case must depend on using an illness or treatment as the explanation for variations in the questioned signature it is wise for the examiner to limit the level of certainty in any opinions expressed. If explanations are going to be offered to support an opinion, then expert medical authority will be necessary.

Disguise

It was explained earlier that in addition to *C*areful, *C*ommon and *C*areless, there is a fourth "C". The fourth style of writing is *C*ontrived—intentionally disguised writing. A contrived writing is the most frequently encountered cause when two writings by the same person show significant differences. Writers of anonymous letters, threats, graffiti, and persons producing request exemplars will at times attempt to disguise their normal writing habits.

Handwriting disguise, like physical disguise, is not subtle. A subject wishing to produce disguised writing must attempt to set aside habits developed over a lifetime. Their goal is to produce writing that in their opinion does not look like their own writing. Subtle changes will not satisfy this need. Subjects wishing to disguise life-long writing habits must somehow create a writing style that does not have their own natural balance of rhythm and form.

To mask identity, the writer alters elemental and secondary aspects of the writing to a degree that affects the writing balance. However, once that balance is distorted, the writer of a contrived style sees little need for further changes. The resultant writing does not show the rhythm/form balance that would normally be associated with the author, but closer examination may well reveal that the writing includes all of the elements of the author's exemplar writings except for one, or perhaps two, key differences.

The most commonly attempted handwriting disguise is a drastic change in the slant of the writing. This change of slant is drastic enough to upset the proportions, and thus the balance of the writing. Persons who normally write with a moderate right slant will often switch to a left slant or, far less often, to an extreme right slant. The second most frequent alteration attempted is to make a drastic change in the size of the writing. Sometimes the writing will be produced in a small and cramped style; other writers will attempt a large and careless looking style. Along with a change of size and slant many writers of disguised signatures will also change the design of one or two characters, usually the capital letters.

After collection of as many NCB and request exemplars as practical, the examiner working with contrived writings can begin to develop a detailed definition of the habits found in each of the elements of comparison. When the range of variation for each of the elements has been defined, the questioned signatures can be compared to that definition element-by-element. When a contrived signature is analyzed in this manner, in most cases it becomes demonstrably clear that the questioned signature is a distorted version of the same writing habits defined by the exemplars. A contrived signature which exhibits natural pen speed will include elements which are generated from a habit too strong to be eradicated.[41]

In the broader sense of handwriting examination, disguise in exemplar writings presents a different problem than does disguise in questioned signatures. In a questioned writing, such as an anonymous letter, the writer must select a disguise which still leaves the writing legible. There is no use of sending an anonymous letter that can't be read. In producing request exemplar writings, the subject trying to disguise his normal writing habits may attempt to satisfy the examiner with a few lines or pages of scrawled pen markings. The examiner, or whomever is taking the request exemplars, should insist on getting examples of each of the three C's, *C*areful, *C*ommon and *C*areless writings. The subject will have a difficult task trying to produce carefully scrawled writing!

When contriving a disguise, some writers will switch from their usual cursive signature to a printed form. A few will use grossly distorted, or tremulously written forms. It is rare for the writer of a contrived text to invent new forms for the characters. Each person carries in memory some inventory of ways to design each letter. In fabricating disguised forms, the writer will select from that mental inventory those designs that are least frequently used, or that have been forgotten to the conscious mind. Disguised signatures, and especially disguised numbers and printing, will look more adolescent, or even juvenile, compared with the subject's usual style.

Disguise will cause the signature to lack the rhythm/form balance of the subject's natural writing. Yet, on close examination, it will be seen that at the elemental level, both writings include the same individualized habits. The writer has merely taken his own, individualized building blocks and tried to assemble them in a nontypical manner.

The examiner who suspects that either the questioned or the exemplar writing includes an attempted disguise, must thoroughly analyze every element of the writings. Such cases require extra care so that

[41]Baker, p. 44.

important, significant differences that should be recognized as indicative of forgery, are not erroneously explained away as disguise.

A perceived difference in an important signature is a common reason for seeking the assistance of a handwriting expert. Knowing why and how to gather reliable exemplars, how to define the subject's normal signature habits and how to accurately weigh the significance and probable causes of signature variations is the essence of what a document examiner must be able to do.

Chapter Eight

CASE RATINGS

Each examination addresses the same hypothesis and the same set of axioms. The hypothesis states that the writer of the subject document (Q1, etc.) is the same person who produced the exemplar writing (Set K1, etc.). Simply stated—Q = K.

Examination of a questioned signature requires making comparisons to test the hypothesis Q = K. If all the axioms are satisfied the examiner concludes that Q does equal K. A report may be written stating that in the examiner's opinion, the questioned signature matches the exemplars.

If, after a thorough examination of a good collection of exemplars the examiner finds one or more of the axioms cannot be satisfied, such as speed, proportions or design do not match the standards, then the critical hypothesis can not be supported. The examiner might then issue a report expressing the opinion that the questioned signature does not match the standards.

When an examiner has reached the opinion that Q does not equal K (Q ≠ K), the next question will be "who produced the nongenuine signature?" Finding the answer to the second question is far more difficult than the first. In fact, in many cases the "who did it" question cannot be answered.[42]

To identify the author of a forged signature, it is necessary that the questioned signature display the forger's own individualized writing habits. If the questioned signature was produced by a tracing technique, it will not be possible to identify who traced it; a tracing does not display any of the forger's own natural writing habits. Similarly, if the questioned signature is a carefully made drawing of the victims true signature, there is no means by which to identify the forger from the habits displayed.

When a forger tries to write at a natural, rapid pen speed, content with an attempt to capture only the pictorial effect of the victim's signature, there is a good chance the questioned signature will include the forger's

[42]Hilton, p. 199.

own rhythm and form habits. In such cases, the handwriting expert will be able to reduce the universe of possible writers to those whose writing habits include the individualized combinations seen in the questioned signature. It is often possible to identify the writer of a simulated, pictorial forgery.

Many credit card and check forgeries are simple forgeries. The writer just writes the victim's name with no attempt to match a model signature. Simple forgeries are examples of the forger's own writing habits, perhaps with some level of contrived changes intended as a mask. It is possible, indeed likely, that an examiner will be able to identify the writer of simple forgeries.

Before attempting to answer the question as to who produced a forged signature, the habits displayed in the signature should be rated as:

A) unique (presenting a balance of speed, proportion, pressure and design that would be very difficult to equal),
B) somewhat individualized, or,
C) too limited or too simple, to support a definite opinion.

At this same point in the investigation the examiner should determine the size and nature of the universe of possible writers. By addressing these questions early, the examiner can explain the limitations of the case to the investigators or to the client.

When an examination of the victim's exemplars has established that a questioned signature is a forgery, rather than ask "who did it," the better question is "who might have done it?" In other words, how can the universe of possible writers be defined? Circumstances surrounding some questioned documents help define the universe of possible writers. For example, embezzlement through misuse of company records and checks requires access to those documents over a period of time; to forge a signature on a will requires knowledge of the estate and an interest in the dispersion of the assets. In both examples the universe of possible writers is reasonably limited and defined. On the other hand, a lost check or credit card might have been used by anyone in the city on that particular day—the universe of possible writers is unlimited.

The universe of possible writers is defined by investigative reasoning and questioning. For example, when the questioned writing is a forged check, the questions to be answered might include: How was control of the check lost? Was it stolen from a business? Was it stolen from a purse? Was it lost in a known area? Was it lost in an area with limited access?

How much time passed between the moment the owner last saw the check and when it was forged or negotiated? The answers to questions such as these will begin to define the size and nature of the universe of possible writers.

As with a physical identification of a criminal, it is necessary to know the size and nature of the universe of possible writers to establish whether or not an identification of the writer is a realistic goal. A simple forgery that presents the examiner with a small sample of a common style of writing might support identification of the forger from a group of fifty or even one hundred possible writers. That same simple forgery probably would not support trying to identify one person from a group of thousands of possible writers. The examiner needs to be aware of the criteria used to define the universe of possible writers and the number of persons estimated to be in that universe.

To support an opinion that an individual wrote a questioned signature, the document examiner must show that the questioned signature matches the exemplar signatures in individualized writing habits *and* that the comparison shows no significant, inexplicable difference in writing habits. Returning to our physical analogy, the opinion would be: "yes, this is the suspect, not a look-alike."

After defining a reasonable universe of possible writers, the examiner is ready to consider the level of individuality displayed in the questioned signatures. Handwriting is a complex activity involving hundreds of combinations of variables. Each person's writing will include both common and individualized elements. It is the personalized combinations and balance of writing rhythms and character designs which is unique. Looking beyond signature examination for a moment, given an adequately large writing sample as the questioned writing, unique rhythm/form patterns would be present in virtually all writings.

However, few questioned signature cases present the examiner with volumes of questioned material. Many cases present only one signature as the subject material. Before attempting to reach an opinion in a case, the examiner needs to evaluate the level of individuality found in the questioned materials and identify the combinations of habits which can be expected to support an identification.

When the questioned signature presents only a limited measure of the writer's habits, it may be impossible to identify the writer. This limitation may result from questioned writing which consists of only a few characters, or only simple rhythms or simply drawn forms with no complex rhythm/form balance. This situation would be similar to a witness who can give a general description of a suspect but cannot offer any individualized details. That witness might look at a number of suspects and find two or more that *look like* the right person.

With this type of case, the examiner will not be able to positively identify the person who produced the questioned writing. Examination of the writings of suspects may, however, establish who did not produce the questioned writing. As with a physical identification, suspects who look like the description will require further investigation, but those who clearly do not fit the description can be eliminated.

An important caution is necessary in this situation. Even if the document examiner has eliminated all known suspects except one, it still is not established that the remaining suspect produced the questioned writing. Unless the evidence drawn *from* the writing will support a definite opinion, the document examiner can report only that the writings show similarities. The examiner can never depend on a truly closed universe of possible writers. To conclude that since every other known suspect has been eliminated the remaining suspect must be the writer, would be reading an opinion *into* the handwriting evidence, not drawing it *from* the writing.

In some cases the examiner must conclude that the questioned writing does not present a unique balance of rhythm and form. As you will recall from chapter four, some writers use such simple, scrawled lines; such slowly drawn signatures; or present such a wide range of variation that their signatures may not establish a basis for identification. Their signatures are so easily imitated no examiner could be certain whether or not any given signature is genuine.

Examiners in private practice who have worked mostly with civil cases or with defense attorneys, are sometimes critical of their government colleagues because of the frequency of inconclusive opinions written in government laboratories. Many of the cases handled in government labs present parameters quite different from those handled in private labs.

When the questioned writing is a common style, brief signature and the universe of possible writers must be considered to be anyone in the same general area on the day in question, "inconclusive" or "inconclusive, with similarities noted" might well be the only opinion which can objectively be supported. Likewise, if the examiner is limited to working with request standards that are contrived or a heavily disguised questioned signature and a large, open universe of possible writers, it is not reasonable to expect a responsible examiner to reach a definitive opinion.

Exemplars, whether NCB or request writings, are rated in the same way as the questioned writings. As a set the exemplars are rated:

A) unique rhythm/form balance;
B) the set defines only individualized rhythm/form habits;
C) the exemplars are too limited to establish a definition of writing habits useful for identification.

For an exemplar set to form that basis for a conclusive opinion the examiner must be satisfied that it presents a definition of writing habits *unique* in the defined universe of possible writers.

Investigators will sometimes have a good, circumstantial case and seek the examiner's findings as the final, and perhaps only, physical evidence. If the examiner allows the universe to be too narrowly defined, the significance of any similarities (i.e., small size or rapid pen speed) found in an examination can be overestimated.

As a rule-of-thumb, when ranking the usefulness of a set of exemplars, it is wise for the examiner to hypothetically assume that the universe of possible writers includes fifty similar writings. For example, if presented with the exemplars showing writing habits of rapid pen speed, small size, and a high degree of pen pressure, the examiner should consider whether, based on past experience, this set of exemplars would stand out in a universe of fifty writings from persons whose writing is small and rapid. In other words, the examiner needs to be specific as to how the exemplars define a unique balance of writing habits. This precaution helps the examiner guard against reducing the universe of possible writers to one.

The final level of certainty of any opinion that might be reached depends upon the individuality of the writing habits displayed in the materials available to the examiner. By objectively deciding the level of individuality in the questioned materials and in each set of exemplars before beginning the comparisons of writing habits the examiner establishes a foundation for a more objective opinion.

Chapter Nine

WORKING WITH COPIES

Often a document examiner will be unable to gain access to original documents. Sometimes originals have been lost. In some anonymous letter cases the original was never received. In any case, where only copies are available, the examiner must work with special care and keep in mind the limitations of working with photocopies.

Any copy produced from the original document is referred to as a first generation copy. Any subsequent copies made using a first generation copy as the source are second generation copies, and so forth. An examiner might use first or second generation copies to build a study board. Enlarged images made as first or second generation copies can be quite useful for this purpose.

Copies that are received as questioned documents present additional problems for the examiner. Why is the original not available? Did the original ever exist? What happened to it? What generation are the copies? Which elements of rhythm and design will it be possible to use for comparison?

The first questions require attention by the investigator or attorney handling the case. The assessment of which elements can be tested using the available copies can be answered by the examiner. The Elements of Comparison in Figure 1 will help the examiner to decide which elements are measurable from the available copies.

Every examination sets out to test the key hypothesis and its axioms. When the work is limited to examination of copies, it is not possible to subject the hypothesis to some of the usual tests. Careful thought must be given to determining which elements of comparison can be compared reliably and which will have to be left untested until the originals are available.

The quality of each copy must be assessed. When working with high quality copies, many of the elements of handwriting can be used to test the hypothesis. The measurement and comparison of the elements of proportion are possible when working with good copies. It is also possible to make judgments about gross forms, variations in design and connective forms. From some copies it is possible to get an impression of the pen speed used to produce the writing. Evidence of either very fast or very slow writing can sometimes be seen in high quality copies. Be careful to not interpret the rough edges on the writing line which may be caused by uneven deposits of toner, as an indicator of slow pen speed.

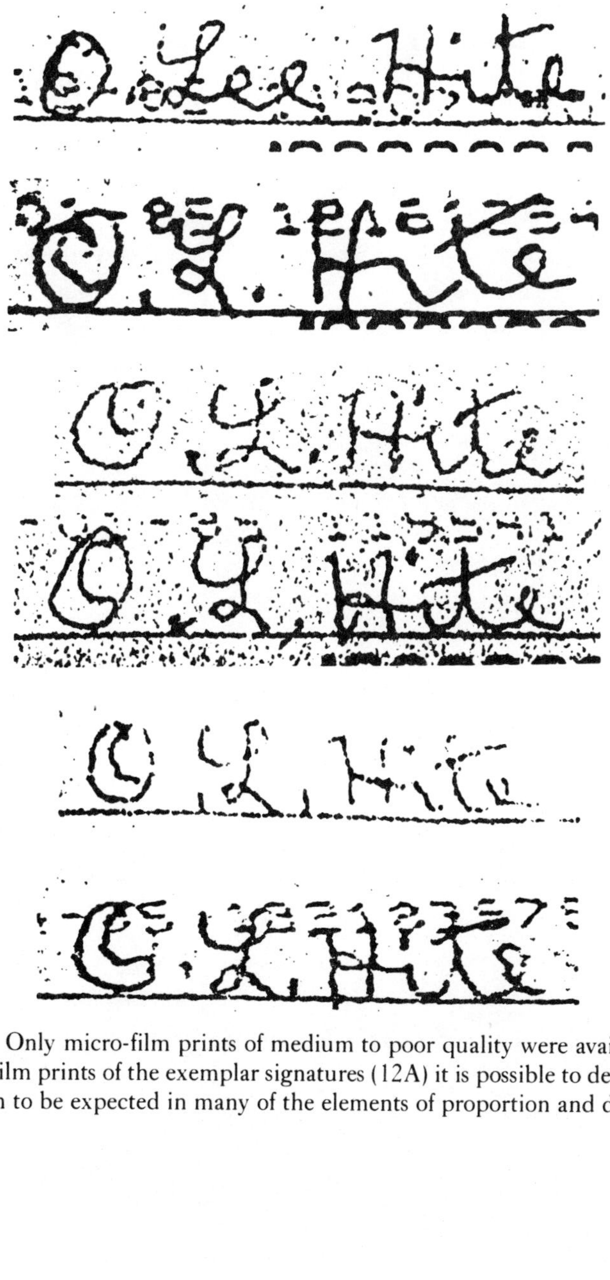

Illustration 12A. Only micro-film prints of medium to poor quality were available for this case. With the micro-film prints of the exemplar signatures (12A) it is possible to define the habits and range of variation to be expected in many of the elements of proportion and design.

J E C T

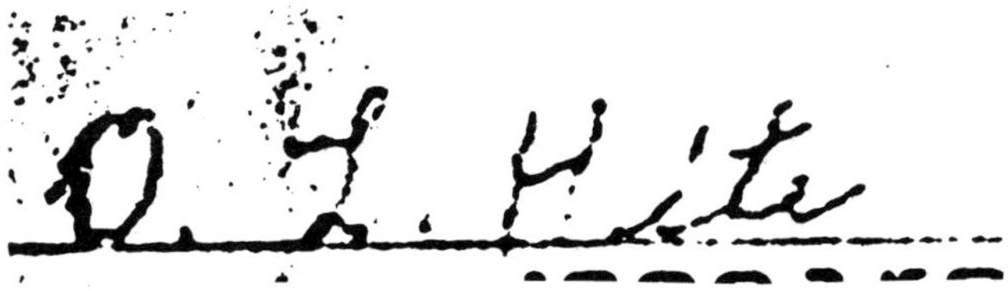

12B.

ELEMENTS OF COMPARISON --WORKSHEET

Case ILLUSTRATION #12

Comparison of Q 12-B ; HITE SIGNATURE

with the Exemplars for(Set K 1) O. L. HITE (12-A)

Ratings: Subject A; (B;) C. Exemplars A; (B;) C. } ALL DOCUMENTS EXAMINED WERE MICROFILM PRINTS.

ELEMENTAL	SECONDARY	PRIMARY	CRITICAL
Ticks & Feather Strokes; Smoothness of Curves; Smoothness of Pressure Changes	Speed (1)	(1) CAN NOT TEST DUE TO LIMITATIONS OF THE MICROFILM PRINTS.	
Placement OK; Expansion & Spacing ≠; Top of Writing (TOW) ≠; Base of Writing (BOW); Angulation/Slant ≠	Proportions ≠	RHYTHMS ≠	
Overall Pressure; Pressure Change Patterns	Pressure (1)		
			RHYTHM/FORM BALANCE ≠
Gross Forms ≠; Variations; Connective Forms ≠ (2); Micro-Forms (1)	Design (2)	FORM ≠	

REMARKS: Q ≠ K. DIFFERENCES OF PROPORTIONS AND DESIGN CAN BE SEEN IN THESE PRINTS.

OPINION/LEVEL OF CERTAINTY: I; II; III; (IV:)

12C.

Illustration 12B&C. Within the limitations of the writing elements which can be reliably defined and compared, it is possible to determine that the subject signature (12B) includes several significant differences of both rhythm and form. The subject signature does not equal the rhythm/form balance defined by the signatures in 12A. (See sample worksheet, Illustration 12C.)

At best, a limited assessment of pressure is possible from copies. Some copies will show the general level of pressure. The varying thickness of the lines of the writing give some indication of pressure modulation patterns. Overall pressure is more difficult to assess.

Many copy machines are sensitive to the color of the ink used on the original. Copies made from writing done with blue ink will not show the same density as copies of the same writing done in black or red ink.

Determining the elements that can be reliably compared depends on the specific copies being examined. Some modern copies are very good, but they are never as reliable as the original document. Copies may be of sufficient quality that the examiner can be certain of a significant difference between the standards and the questioned materials in one or more of the elements of comparison. By an examination of copies it may be possible to ascertain that one or more of the axioms, and thus the key hypothesis, is not supported, i.e., the examiner can see significantly different proportions, differences in design or even evidence of clumsy drawing or tracing in a copy. When that is true, the examiner may say with certainty that the questioned writing does not match the exemplars.

Elements which can be reliably tested and which show that the questioned writing does not match the standards will allow a conclusion that Q does not equal K. However, since copies will not allow full testing of every element it is not possible to reach such a high level of certainty that Q does equal K. Until every element can be examined so that all of the axioms can be as completely tested as possible, the examiner will have to express a limited or conditional opinion. When writing a report for an examination based on copies, the examiner should reserve the privilege of being allowed to verify the accuracy of the copies if the original documents become available.

The growing popularity of facsimile machines is presenting document examiners with another set of problems. Fax copies show characteristic scan or raster lines. The quality of a fax copy depends on the quality of the sending machine, the connection between the machines and the quality of the receiving machine. If enlarged copies of the signatures can be made before they are transmitted, the fax images will be more useful to the examiner. Image quality is being steadily improved. Machines which transmit directly between computers and machines with laser printers are producing images that can be useful for initial examinations.

The usefulness of facsimile copies for identification purposes can be assessed in the same manner as that described for photocopies. Because the scanning raster breaks up the continuous lines of the writing, writing speed and the presence of pen lifts cannot be assessed from fax copies. The examiner should not rely on fax copies. If preliminary work must be done using high quality fax copies, the originals should subsequently be examined before any findings or opinions are expressed.

With modern copying equipment it is simple to create a copy of a document that never existed as an original. Signatures can be inserted into contracts. Whole pages of writing can be composed using handwritten words from sources available to a person willing to commit such a fraud. Using a computer equipped with an input-scanning system, it is now possible to create copies of documents that are virtually flawless—except that no true original ever existed.

The examiner must check each document carefully. A contract which appears to be a black and white, typed original signed with blue ink, may, in fact, be a color copy with the image of a blue ballpoint pen signature inserted to give the appearance of a genuine original document.

Copies need not be an unworkable limitation in a case. They are certainly further reason for the examiner to work with systematic thoroughness and caution.

Chapter Ten

OPINION—LEVELS OF CERTAINTY

After the universe of possible writers has been decided, the exemplar sets assembled and the range of variation in each element and in the rhythm/form balance has been defined, the examiner can begin the first comparison between a questioned signature and a set of exemplars. As the analysis of the evidence proceeds, the key hypothesis Q = K is either supported or contradicted. Eventually the examination of each set of exemplars will lead the expert to an opinion at one of four possible levels of certainty. The four possible levels are:

Level I:	Q equals K—beyond any reasonable doubt.
Level II:	It is highly probable that Q = K.
Level III:	Inconclusive (or, inconclusive with similarities noted).
Level IV:	It is demonstrably clear that Q does not equal K.

Criteria for a Conclusive Match or Level I Opinion

At Level I, the examiner is reporting that the writer of the exemplar materials is, in the examiner's professional opinion, beyond any reasonable doubt, also the writer of the questioned materials. Such a positive opinion may be expressed when the following criteria are met:

- The questioned writing or questioned signature presents a combination of rhythms and forms which the examiner regards as unique.
- The exemplar collection provides a basis for a fair and reasonable definition of the subject's range of normal variation and defines a unique rhythm/form balance.
- The habits seen in the questioned materials match the individualized habits of rhythm/form balance defined by the exemplars with no significant difference. (The comparisons show that the evidence satisfies the axioms set out in Chapter Two.)

In most cases the criteria for a Level I opinion can be met. There are cases in which limitations can not be overcome and therefore, a Level I opinion can not be supported.

Criteria for a Limited or Level II Opinion

A Level II opinion means that in the examiner's professional opinion it is highly probable that the writer of the exemplars also produced the writings in question. A Level II opinion can also be referred to as a qualified opinion or a limited opinion. When an examination ends at this level of certainty it is due to some limitation in the case which the examiner has not been able to overcome.

The limited or qualified opinion will require a thorough explanation if the case reaches the point that testimony is to be taken from the expert. At this level of certainty the examiner is saying that the Q = K hypothesis has not been fully tested. The reasons why testing was limited will need to be carefully explained. Possible causes for a Level II opinion include:

- A limited amount of questioned writing.
- Questioned writing that is disguised.
- Questioned writing that was written to imitate the victim's writing habits.
- A victim's exemplars show an extremely wide range of normal variation, presenting a forger with an easy target.
- A victim's exemplars show a lack of rhythm/form balance due to a signature style which is either simple rhythms with no complex design or, easily produced character designs with no complex integration of rhythms.
- It has not been possible to assemble an adequate collection of exemplar materials to fairly define either the victim's or the subject's range of normal variation.

In reporting a limited opinion, the examiner is saying that based on the quantity and/or quality of the materials made available for the examination, it appears significantly more probable than not that the writer of the exemplars is the writer of the questioned materials.

Attorneys, especially opposing attorneys, like to have probabilities expressed as percentages. In that form of expression a Level II opinion might range from 60 to 90 percent certain that the subject writing is by the same person who produced the exemplars. That expression means that the examiner has been able to satisfactorily test the key hypothesis (Q = K) by a comparison of 60 to 90 percent of the elements that can be tested (Figure One), and that for all of those tests the hypothesis stands.

On cross examination the examiner should expect that the opposing attorney will try to reinterpret a 90 percent level of certainty as meaning there is one chance in ten that the opinion is not correct. That would not be the correct interpretation of that expression. The best response to this line of questioning is to explain that: The hypothesis that Q = K might be shown to be false only if there proved to be a significant difference of habit in the 10 percent of the testing which it has not been possible to complete.

Criteria for an Inconclusive or Level III Opinion

When the examiner has conducted a thorough examination of adequate subject (Q) and exemplar (K) materials and finds it is not possible to adequately test the key hypothesis Q = K the correct opinion to be reported is "inconclusive." Examples of cases which might be expected to end with inconclusive findings include:

- Cases in which the subject writing does not present enough identifiers to support a thorough examination. This limitation might be due to the limited quantity of questioned writing, a questioned writing that only presents a brief example of a simple or common writing style or a questioned writing produced in a heavily disguised style. Cases in which the questioned writing presents only an extremely brief signature, simple initials, or one or two words on a note might be examples.
- Cases in which the range of variation in the habits of the writer cannot be established. This limitation might be due, among other reasons, to a lack of NCB standards for a deceased writer or the inability to get request writings which repeat a contrived style.
- And, cases in which the exemplars show that the subject's writing habits are so simple or vary to such a degree that it is an easy task to imitate his or her writings.

When a questioned writing shows some individualized combinations of habits which are also seen in the exemplars, but the materials available to the examiner are not sufficient to support a thorough examination, the examiner might then report "inconclusive, with similarities noted." If more materials become available, the case could be reexamined.

Criteria for a Conclusive Nonmatch or Level IV Opinion

A Level IV opinion means the examiner has conducted a thorough examination and concluded that Q does not equal K. Or, "The writer of the exemplar materials (K) is not the writer of the subject signature (Q)." The criteria for a Level IV opinion are:

- The questioned writing displays writing habits significantly different from those defined by a fair and reasonable collection of exemplars.
- There is no reasonable explanation for the differences.

The methods described so far in this work allow the examiner to conduct a signature comparison with a high degree of objectivity. Before the comparison of a questioned signature begins, the examiner has ranked the individuality of that signature (A, B, or C) and ranked the individuality of the exemplar sets to be used (A, B, or C). The key hypothesis and axioms have been stated. The thresholds of significance for any differences have been defined (Elemental, Secondary, Primary, and Critical). And, the criteria for reaching a conclusion have been stated. By following these steps in a disciplined manner, the scientific method has been applied to the comparison of signature habits.

Chapter Eleven

ERRORS

Document examiners must conduct each forensic analysis from a neutral, objective point of view. It is not the document examiner's responsibility to prove a point for either side. The examiner's role is to perform an objective, professional examination. In private practice, if the outcome of the analysis does not support the interests of the parties who paid for the work, then the examiner is probably finished working on that case. In law enforcement, the examiner may go on to examine writing samples from other suspects or go on to the next case. For both the private examiner and the law enforcement examiner, the work must be done without any attempt to reconcile objective findings with other evidence or opinions.

When the examiner's findings and opinion do support the position of the client, then expert testimony may be used as an element in the client's advocacy. The examiner, however, must remain neutral in the overall case. It is never the document examiner's responsibility to "win" a case. That is the attorney's job.

The examiner will be called on to prepare exhibits which illustrate the comparisons made, and the reasons for the opinions being offered. Every well-trained examiner should be able to clearly communicate the methods used for the examination and the specific details which led to the reported opinion. The opposing side of the case may produce another examiner who has reached an opposite opinion. With or without its own expert, the opposition's task is to convince the court, or at least a few jurors, that the expert who is testifying should not be believed.

Honest and objective minds can disagree. Unfortunately, some document examiners are not always objective in their work. I believe some are even dishonest. And, personal and political issues can effect an examiner's perspective. Whenever a document examiner fails to work with an open and objective mind the critics who label all expert witnesses as hired guns are given credibility.

Document examiners train themselves to make objective, critical judgments about document evidence. Among well-trained, experienced examiners, errors are rare. Nonetheless, document examiners are human, and document examination is not an exact science. Even when working with a high degree of objectivity misjudgments can be made. Most errors made by document examiners result from a misjudgment in:

- the size or nature of the universe of possible writers.
- the level of individuality defined by either the questioned writing or the exemplar writing.
- defining the range of normal variation in the subject's rhythm and form habits.
- the significance of a difference found between the questioned and exemplar materials.
- the validity of a theory offered to explain the differences between the questioned and exemplar materials.

These factors are the common denominators in errors made by document examiners. In the presence of doubt about any of the aspects listed above, the examiner should report that the materials will only support a limited opinion or report inconclusive results.

A misjudgment by an examiner can have one of three results. It might lead to an inconclusive result in a case with sufficient evidence to support a more decisive opinion. Or, the examiner might incorrectly report that the questioned signature or writing does not match the exemplars (a false negative result). Or, the examiner might incorrectly report that a questioned writing does match the exemplars (a false positive result). Any error is a serious matter.

False Negative Errors

An examiner may incorrectly decide that two signatures, or two writings, are not by the same person. False negative opinions can cause wills or contracts to come into costly dispute, when the signatures are, in fact, authentic. Or, false negatives can mean that a person responsible for a fraud is dismissed from prosecution.

Overestimating the significance of some slight difference found in a questioned signature is probably the most common error made by document examiners. Errors of this nature are often the cause of contradictory testimony by experts. Such errors occur when an examiner accepts an isolated, elemental difference as proof that a disputed signature was not produced by the same person who produced the exemplars.

It is not reasonable to expect that any set of exemplars will illustrate every possible variation that a subject's writing might include. An elemental difference in proportions of a letter, a false start or interruption, a single slowing of pen speed or a minor variation in the way a character was formed does not, by itself, prove a signature is a forgery. An opinion that a questioned signature does not match the exemplars is even more difficult to support when an examiner is working with request exemplars.

If the overall rhythm/form balance in the questioned signature is within the range defined by the exemplars, an isolated element that varies slightly is not significant. In many instances, additional exemplar materials would broaden the definition of the subject's writing habits enough to include the difference in question. Certainly, before an examiner reports a signature to be a forgery based solely on an isolated, elemental difference, the examiner should make an extensive search for more exemplars. Saying that an elemental difference proves a signature is not genuine is equal to arguing for the dismissal of a defendant because his hair is now combed in a different style than that originally described by a witness.

When an examiner finds a question signature to not be within the rhythm/form parameters defined by the exemplars, but is faced with some plausible explanation for those differences, rejecting that explanation might lead to a false negative error. The examiner may not be qualified to judge the validity of the explanation. Indeed, there may be no one who is qualified to do so.

Almost no reliable research has been done into the effects of diseases, medications, alcohol, trauma, and aging on writing skills. What well designed research is available indicates that examiners and the courts must be careful in making any assumptions about how handwriting skills might be influenced by any of these factors.

When an explanation for some distortion in a signature is being offered, the prudent document examiner will conduct a careful study and make an informed judgment as the plausibility of that explanation. It might be necessary to consult with medical or other experts. In such cases a limited opinion or inconclusive findings are in order.

False Positive Errors

False positive errors can cause an innocent person to be prosecuted, or they can cause a forged instrument to be enforced. Most false positive errors result from the examiner's failure to recognize that the signature in question presents a forger with an easy task. This situation might be the result of a rhythm/form balance that is at one extreme or the other, or a range of normal variation so wide that the exemplars include virtually any errors a forger might make.

The misjudgments that most often lead to false positive opinions are an erroneous assessment of the level of individuality defined by the exemplar signatures, or, failure to properly assess the level of individuality presented in the questioned writings. Failure to properly rate the individuality presented in the questioned and/or exemplar materials can lead the examiner to a positive opinion based only on the presence of common handwriting characteristics. The examiner has then taken what are commonly found elements of handwriting and judged them to be sufficiently individualized to support an identification. An analogy would be to prosecute someone who happens to fit the general description of the criminal.

False positive opinions also result from errors in judging the size or nature of the universe of possible writers. If the document examiner allows the universe of possible writers to be too narrowly defined, then the individuality of handwriting characteristics can be overestimated. This problem most frequently occurs when an investigator wants to know if the writing of a suspect can be matched to the questioned signatures. If the examiner allows the universe of possible writers to be reduced to one, the importance of any matching points can be overestimated. The examiner may feel some pressure to take the investigators' circumstantial evidence into account.

The examiner faced with such a situation needs to take steps to guard against making a false positive error. Before expressing an opinion, the examiner should hypothetically consider whether the writing being examined is sufficient in quantity and individuality to separate it from a large collection of generally similar writings. For example, if the subject writing is of moderate size with a moderate right slant, what would allow that subject's writing to be separated from fifty other writing samples showing moderate size and moderate right slant?

If the materials being examined would not support the premise that the subject's writing would be unique in a pool of fifty, generally similar writings, the examiner should express a limited opinion.

Another cause of false positive errors is the acceptance of an invalid explanation for differences between the questioned and exemplar materials. Examiners need to be skeptical of explanations. If the examiner does not do a thorough job of seeking all possible exemplars, and does not seek assistance in judging the credibility of any explanations, it is possible to be steered toward a false positive opinion.

Chapter Twelve

REPORTS

Examiners working for a government agency will prepare at least a brief report for every case examined. In private practice, many cases will end with only a verbal report to the client, or to the client's attorney.

In private practice, it is common for attorneys to first engage a document examiner as a consultant. Hired on a consulting basis, the examiner's findings and opinions can be shielded from discovery by the other side of the case. This allows the attorney to gather information and plan an approach to the case that best serves their client, without revealing adverse findings to the opposition. If the examiner's opinion does not support the client's interests in the case, the examiner's work may end with a verbal report. Once hired by a client, even if the examination leads to an opinion which goes against the client's interests, the examiner is ethically blocked from working on the case for the opposing side. Any contact by other parties to the case should be referred to the original client's counsel.

When the opinion reached does support the client's case, the attorney will name the expert when filing a witness list and a written report may be requested. The examiner's written report will be shared with the attorney representing the opposing side of the case. If the parties believe a settlement might be reached, the report, along with all the other evidence the attorneys have gathered, will play a part in the settlement negotiations.

In preparing a written report, the examiner should try to be matter-of-fact and informative. How the examiner prefers to write reports is a matter of personal choice. Whatever the examiner's preferred style, reports need to follow a general outline and cover the following information:

- Who requested the examination.
- What documents were examined.
- What purposes the examination sought to address.
- What was found through the examination.

- What opinions were reached.
- The level of certainty the examiner gives to those opinions.
- What has become of the materials examined.
- The current status of the examiner's file.

Who requested the report is easily addressed in the opening paragraph. The materials examined can be described in two sections, the subject materials are identified in some detail and labeled as Q1, Q2, etc. The exemplars can be identified individually or in sets. Exemplars from the normal course of business should be identified as "the purported writings of . . . " only when the examiner has personally witnessed the request writings produced by a suspect should the report include a statement such as "the writings of . . . "

The report should include a statement of purpose. This statement paraphrases the hypothesis of the examination and spells out what the examiner sought to do. An example might be: This examination was conducted in an attempt to determine whether the habits of writing rhythm and character design displayed in subject Q1 match the habits defined by the signatures in exemplar Set K1.

With the materials identified and the hypothesis stated, the examiner's report then explains the findings of the examination. This section of the report must be written so that it clearly informs the reader. However, it does not need to be educational. The findings from the examination can be expressed clearly without going into an element-by-element or stroke-by-stroke analysis of the writings examined. When the case progresses to trial the examiner will be able to use exhibits and explain the definition and comparison of every element of the writings. It is not necessary or desirable to try to do so in a written report. The expression of the examiner's findings can be clearly presented by answering the following questions:

- How did the examiner assess the individuality of the questioned signature or writings? (A, B or C—Chapter Eight.)
- How did the examiner assess the usefulness of the exemplars? (A, B or C—Chapter Eight.)
- What, if any, are the factors which handicapped the examination or limited the certainty of the examiner's opinion? (Chapter Ten.)
- What was found when the subject writing was compared with the habits defined by the exemplars? (Habits match? Habits nearly match? Habits do not match?)

- What explanations have been offered to explain any differences between the habits defined by the exemplars and those seen in the subject writing? Was that explanation accepted or rejected?

Once the report has answered these questions, the examiner's opinion can be expressed. If the examiner believes the materials have satisfied the requirements of a Level I opinion, the report can state, "It is my opinion, beyond any reasonable doubt, that the writer of the documents in exemplar set K1 also produced the signature identified in this report as subject Q1."

If the materials examined only satisfy the requirements of a Level II opinion (page 70), that fact should be made clear with language such as "it is my limited opinion" or "it is my opinion that it is highly probable that . . . " It is not necessary to explain the reasons for reporting a limited opinion in full detail in the report. The report should include a summary statement such as "due to limited exemplar materials" or "due to the wide range of normal variations," which tells the reader the general nature of the limitations encountered in the examination.

The report for an examination limited by any of the factors discussed in conjunction with the explanations for a Level III opinion (page 71) should simply state that the findings are inconclusive. In some cases an examiner will need to report that the examination was inconclusive " . . . with similarities noted . . . "

Of course, when an examiner is certain that the writings in question do not match the exemplars, the report so states. (See criteria for Level IV opinion, page 72.)

There are some words or phrases which are best avoided in written reports. Attorneys, certainly opposing attorneys, can spend a great deal of time—and can make an examiner uncomfortable on the witness stand—by tediously dissecting every word and phrase in a report. The definition of forgery includes language pertaining to the issue of "with purpose to defraud";[43] it is best to not use the word "forgery" in reports or testimony. It is sufficient to report that the questioned signature does not match the writing habits defined by the exemplars. By avoiding the term *forgery* when writing or speaking for the record, the examiner avoids a line of cross-examination into how he or she was able to divine the writer's intentions. Lawyers make arguments out of adjectives—there is no reason to give them an adjective such as *forged* to work with.

---

[43]Black, Henry Campbell. *Black's Law Dictionary,* Fifth Edition. St. Paul, West, 1979, p. 585.

Another term that must be used with care is *questioned document.* In testimony or as a label on exhibits, referring to a document as questioned conveys a sense that something is presumed to be wrong with it. Exhibits will be better accepted and testimony more smoothly delivered when the term *subject document* is used.

An examiner needs to avoid saying anything beyond what is necessary to adequately address the immediate need. Writing reports in simple, plain language with no embellishments will result in easier testimony.

The last section of the report is used for discussion of any points the examiner or the attorney think should be explained. These points might include an explanation of the problems caused by working with the copies that were available, a request to see originals for any copies that were used, or a request for additional exemplars to help resolve a Level II or III finding. The discussion paragraphs should tell the reader what has been done to either maintain or return the materials examined. And, the discussion paragraphs should explain the status of the examiner's file as of the date of the report. For example, the examiner might state that all documents examined were photocopied and photographed before being returned. The examiner might further state that the file contains photonegatives and, when necessary, exhibits will be prepared and testimony given in support of the opinions reported.

Chapter Thirteen

TESTIMONY–TRIALS AND DEPOSITIONS

Only a small percentage of cases require the document examiner to present testimony. Document examiners working in either a civil or a criminal case may be called upon to present testimony in open court. Some cases will be heard only by a judge; others will require testimony before a jury. An examiner working on a civil case might also be required to give testimony in a deposition.

The written report was meant to inform the reader. At a trial and in most depositions, testimony should be given in a manner that will educate the court as to the methods used in the examination and the reasoning by which an opinion was reached.

Pretrial Preparation

The examiner's work will be of greater value to the client when the examiner and the client's attorney work together. It is through sworn testimony that the examiner's work becomes a part of the official record. The examiner is not an advocate for the client's case. By the time a case is prepared for trial, the examiner will have completed an objective examination of the writings at issue and reached an opinion based on that evidence. In most cases, a report will have been written and submitted to the opposing side through discovery. Preparing for the presentation of testimony is an important step. Some attorneys don't give this step enough attention. Testimony is more effective when the expert and the attorney have developed a set of questions to bring out the expert's qualifications and opinions clearly. The examiner is not advocating or arguing the case by making a strong, clear, and convincing presentation.[44]

The pretrial meeting provides an opportunity to decide which of the examiner's findings and opinions are most important to the attorney's

[44]Baker, p. 150.

case. Questions for direct testimony and the details of the exhibits should be discussed.

Good trial preparation also includes a discussion of any expected challenges to the expert's qualifications. It will be the opposing attorney's task to attack the expert's working methods and opinions. It will be necessary to prepare to deal with that attack. During pretrial preparation, the hiring attorney should play the role of devil's advocate to prepare for some of the probable questions that will be asked during cross-examination.

Particularly in jury trials, it is important to give clear and detailed testimony using any exhibits that will help explain the expert's work for the jury. Resist any temptation to offer "trust me, I know best . . . " testimony. Such testimony is presented without exhibits and with no attempt to explain the comparison process used, or the reasoning which lead to the opinions being offered. It is an arrogant and patronizing insult to the jurors. A well-prepared opposing attorney will often be able to turn a jury against an expert who adopts such an attitude.

Exhibits

Exhibits are simple visual aids that help the expert explain the processes and facts behind an opinion. If testimony is to be presented only to a judge, the exhibits might be a simple handout. The court would be given the original exhibit. The expert should have copies of the exhibit available for each of the attorneys on both sides of the case.

The court is accustomed to looking at evidence and to the methods and requirements for forming opinions. Long, educational presentations are seldom needed or wanted in bench trials. When the case requires a presentation before a jury, an examiner prepares more detailed exhibits. The exhibits help hold the jurors' attention and also allow them to understand exactly how the examiner reached the opinion being presented.

Juror's are intelligent people who are fulfilling a critical role in the legal system. They want and deserve to see the methods and reasoning an expert has followed, and to learn how the opinions being expressed were reached. Jurors want to decide for themselves whether the expert's methods and opinions make sense.

To better meet the juror's needs, the examiner should build a set of exhibits which illustrate the specific points which led to the opinions being offered. The exhibits do not need to show every detail of the documents examined. They are used to assist the expert in making an easily understood explanation of how the case was handled and the reasoning processes applied to the evidence.

There are many methods for presenting an exhibit to a jury. For example, images of signatures might be projected onto a screen for viewing. Slides, overhead transparencies, video or projection directly from the original documents might be used to enlarge the images and bring the jurors' attention to the points the examiner wants to discuss. Projection techniques have the advantage of allowing the examiner to make the images as large as necessary without making photographic enlargements. However, there are drawbacks to the use of projection methods.

Equipment which needs to be set up and adjusted will interrupt the flow of the case and waste the court's time. Any malfunction or difficulties with equipment, electrical supplies, or the brightness of the room lights can severely handicap a presentation. If it becomes necessary to refer back to a slide or transparency presented earlier, the examiner runs the risk of fumbling around until the correct image is located. If an expert does have trouble relocating an image, the opposing attorney will be unable to resist frustrating the expert further by requesting to reexamine several images in hopes of causing embarrassment and confusion.

It is also helpful to the jury to review and study the expert's exhibits during their deliberations. If projected images are used in court, the expert needs to make provisions for the exhibits to be duplicated as hard copies so that they can be entered into the record and given to the jury to consider.

In most cases, the best exhibits are those prepared using photographs mounted on exhibit boards. Unless there is some special reason to make color photographs, black-and-white enlargements make satisfactory exhibits. A set of high quality, black-and-white enlargements are not a great expense when compared to what is at stake in any jury trial.

Generally, enlargements from five to ten diameters are satisfactory. For example, a signature which is three inches long on the original document would be enlarged to a length of from fifteen to as much as thirty inches for the exhibits. The subject signature and each exemplar signature selected for the exhibit should be enlarged by the same factor. The expert will refer to the enlarged exemplars to explain the writer's normal rhythm/form habits and range of normal variation. The reasons why the examiner believes the questioned signature does or does not match the habits defined by the exemplars will be evident as the jury follows the explanation and sees the details in the photographs for themselves. Where a lengthy explanation would confuse and bore jurors, a good exhibit engages them in the comparison process. An effective exhibit and a logical explanation make a convincing combination.[45] Later, when the jury deliberates the case they often spend time reviewing the exhibits and discussing the examiner's testimony in detail.

Direct Testimony

During direct testimony the attorney who hired the examiner asks questions designed to present the examiner's findings and opinions to the court. As a general outline, direct testimony consists of qualifying the expert, asking whether the expert has conducted an examination relevant to the case before the court, asking what opinions the expert has reached, and then asking how those opinions were reached. When asked how the opinion was reached, the expert should use the exhibits and any other visual aids necessary to help the jurors understand the methods used and the findings and reasoning which led to the opinions offered.

The written report was used to inform everyone of the experts opinion. Direct testimony, especially in a jury trial, is the time to teach the jury the methods used and the reasoning which supports the expert's opinion.[46] In many cases I have used an enlargement of the Elements of Comparison (Figure One) when testifying in a jury trial. The chart makes the relative importance of the elements of comparison clear to the jurors. Using Figure One, together with enlargements of the subject and exemplar materials, it is possible to teach jurors what to look for and how to weigh the importance of the elements in a handwriting comparison.[47] At the end of the examiner's presentation, the client's attorney will again ask to have the opinions restated for the jury. After direct presentation, the court will instruct the expert to answer questions from the opposing attorney.

---

[45]Baker, p. 149.

[46]Baker, p. 148.

[47]Baker, p. 98.

Cross Examination

The Constitution guarantees the right to face our accusers. Cross examination is the opposing attorney's opportunity to exercise that right for a client. There are two broad avenues open to the opposing attorney; one or both might be pursued. Questioning may attempt to minimize the weight the jury gives to the examiner's testimony by attacking the examiner's credentials. Questions might also be asked in an attempt to raise doubt about the accuracy of the examiner's work.

Testimony is sometimes taken in two separate phases—presentation of the examiner's qualifications with cross-examination on qualifications only (voir dire), and then presentation of the examiner's opinions, followed by cross-examination on that testimony.

If an opposing attorney believes it may be possible to block the testimony by preventing the court from accepting the examiner as an expert, the cross-examination on qualifications will be conducted before any technical evidence or opinions are expressed. When an opposing attorney believes it might be possible to disqualify an expert, voir dire may involve aggressive questioning. Being cross-examined by an aggressive, skilled attorney is never a comfortable experience, but there are a few guidelines to help the expert witness.

Do not answer if you don't know. This may seem obvious, but when facing an attorney who is trying to make you look incompetent, it can be difficult to say "I don't know" in response to what seems like a minor question. Attorneys will sometimes try to set a trap with what seems to be a line of unimportant questions. For example, "Have you ever heard of or read any of the papers published by Mr. Smith, the most important document examiner in the XYZ Laboratories?" After studying the publications of examiners from all over the country and meeting examiners at technical seminars, the expert might feel fairly certain that Mr. Smith's name is familiar. There is some basis and a certain temptation to answer the question affirmatively. But, unless the expert truly knows Mr. Smith, knows what his position is at XYZ Labs and can recall at least one of the papers he has published, then "I don't know" is the only appropriate response. Bear in mind that while the witness is under oath, the attorney is not. There is always the possibility that there is no Mr. Smith and possibly no XYZ Labs. If the expert goes for the bait, the room will soon become ten degrees too warm!

Take time to think before answering. Even on seemingly simple questions, such as your address, for which the answer is clear and simple, pause for a few seconds before speaking. Do not let the attorney establish such a rapid question and answer pace that the likelihood of an erroneous statement is increased. Take time to think about exactly what was asked and choose the wording of the answer carefully. Remember that once testimony is on the record, it is reduced to only the words. The record does not reflect the time taken to think before answering.

Choose your words carefully. The expert must be certain that the words chosen express a point and mean exactly what is intended. As with bait and trap questions the expert must resist an opposing attorney's attempts to switch the meaning of the testimony by using so-called "synonymous" terms.

Keep your answers short and to the specific point, do not volunteer any more information than it takes to answer the question. The more the expert says, the more fuel the attorney has for further questioning.

Don't overstate any point. Never inflate the extent or importance of your training or any part of your preparation for working as a document examiner. The only reason a document expert is put on the stand is to give the jury the benefit of that expert's special knowledge and skills as they have been applied to the case being tried. The expert must be credible or the effect of that testimony is lost. Conservative, factual responses that do not exaggerate any point will give the expert the greatest credibility with the jury. Sometimes, on direct testimony, an attorney will try to pressure an expert to state an opinion just a little more strongly or with a little more certainty than the evidence supports. The expert must resist that pressure. To overstate any point will cause the expert's testimony to be less credible.

As with cross-examination on credentials, cross-examination on the reasoning and methods an examiner used in reaching an opinion can also be aggressive. It is at this point during testimony that an opposing attorney might raise questions about the documents used as exemplars or the analytical methods the examiner employed. Frequently attorneys will point out minor differences or similarities, depending on their client's interest, and ask the expert whether or not these points were considered in the examination. Most often the attorney will be attempting to discredit the expert's opinion on the basis of the smallest, elemental difference. Referring to the chart in Figure One to answer such questions allows the expert to keep minor, elemental differences in perspective for the jury.

As the expert's testimony begins to wind down, the witness will again be asked questions by the hiring attorney. This phase, referred to as redirect, allows the attorney to try to rebuild any part of the testimony damaged on cross-examination or clarify any area that seems confusing. After redirect there will be a recross in which the opposing attorney may ask questions to address any points raised on redirect. This process of redirect and recross may go on for some time. It is common for the judge or even jurors to be allowed to ask questions before the expert is dismissed. These phases of the questioning process are just as important as the earlier direct testimony. The expert must stay alert and answer each question thoughtfully.

Depositions

Document examiners who work on civil cases will frequently be asked to present testimony in a deposition. A deposition is sworn testimony and becomes a part of the formal record. The deposition may be taken as a part of discovery by the opposing side of the case, or it might be taken by the hiring attorney to preserve the expert's testimony. Do not be lulled into any false sense that the deposition is not as critical as trial testimony. During the deposition the opposing attorney will have an opportunity to examine the expert's files and working notes. Copies of those papers may be made exhibits to the deposition. In addition to the worksheets and notes from the examiner's file, every spoken word will be on the record and later, if there is any discrepancy between the expert's trial testimony and what was recorded at the deposition, that discrepancy will be exploited by the opposing attorney.

In some cases, usually due to circumstances of time, travel, or cost, the expert's deposition will be presented at trial instead of having the expert present in person. Depositions that are recorded on videotape are becoming more popular as a substitute for having the expert appear at trial. Video depositions allow the attorney to reduce travel costs, waiting time costs, and scheduling problems. However, much of the value of expert testimony is lost when the jury sees only a videotape. When presenting live testimony, the expert can make eye contact with jurors and respond to even a questioning look. When in touch with the members of the jury, the expert is able to work more effectively to help each juror understand the testimony. In many courts, a juror who has a question about the expert's work will be allowed to ask that question—obviously impossible with a videotaped witness.

Depositions that are to be used in lieu of live testimony will require at least small, simple exhibits and will follow the lines of trial testimony. The expert will be questioned by attorneys for both sides of the case.

When a deposition is taken as a part of the opposing attorney's discovery, the questioning will usually be conducted by the opposing attorney and will, in most respects, follow the lines of a cross-examination. The expert does not need to prepare exhibits for such a deposition.

Chapter Fourteen

QUESTIONING THE DOCUMENT EXAMINER

Direct examination of a questioned document examiner is a straightforward process. The first hurdle for the attorney is to have the court recognize the witness as a qualified expert. Once accepted as qualified, the expert is permitted to express an *opinion* about the evidence. For the technical skills of a document examiner to be of value, the examiner must be able to make a logical and persuasive presentation before the court. The expert's exhibits and technical testimony must allow the court to understand the methods and reasoning that led to the opinion. The direct presentation must be convincing, but at the same time the expert should not appear to be reaching too far or acting as an advocate.

Cross-examination of the handwriting expert is critical to the attorneys on both sides of the issue. The following questions are intended to help opposing attorneys design an effective cross-examination for the handwriting expert. The attorney whose case is being supported by the expert's testimony might use this section to play the role of devil's advocate to help prepare the examiner for cross-examination.

A well-trained examiner who knows the literature in the field and has been through some court experience will be able to deal effectively with questions such as those to be presented here. For some of these questions, such as those asking for sources of reliable, published research, there is no satisfactory answer. A knowledgeable expert will not base an opinion on untested ideas. If an expert has done so, that fact should be brought out before the court.

In document examination, as in everything else, experience counts for a great deal. Decades of experience working with signatures does build a body of knowledge that is reliable even if it is not documented in formal papers or studies. In some situations, an expert can effectively cite personal or professional experience in explaining the reasons for differences between signatures. Citing experience should not be abused, however, or it will sound as if the examiner is ducking the hard questions.

Cross-examination of Qualifications

Cross-examination of the examiner's qualifications naturally begins with questions relating to training and experience. Sample questions—education:

- Please describe your formal education and any degrees you hold.
- How do your degrees relate to document examination?
- Other than document examination, what training or professional experience have you had in a technical field?

Sample questions—document examination training:

- How did you begin your training to become a document examiner? With whom did you study? Was this an apprenticeship?
- How many hours did you spend with this person each week or month?
- What was the training and background of the person with whom you studied?
- How many years did you spend doing independent, self-study in document examination?

Sample questions—affiliations and certification testing:

- Are you affiliated with any technical groups for document examiners? Which ones? For how long?
- Does that group require you to pass any tests or peer reviews before being granted membership?
- Does that group offer a certification program?
- Have you been certified by that program?
- Did you get your certification through a grandfather clause?
- Did your certification require written testing?
- Who designed the tests?
- Were those tests administered under supervised conditions?
- Were you allowed to take the tests at home through the mail?
- Could a document examiner who is not a member of your group, apply to take those tests? Why? Why not?
- Was any of your test work reviewed by anyone other than the members of your own group?
- Do you have to be retested periodically in order to maintain your certified status? How often?
- If not, why not?

- Does the group with which you are associated hold any training seminars? How often?
- How many of these have you attended?
- How long are these seminars?
- How many hours of class time are offered at each seminar?
- How much of that is devoted to forensic signature examination techniques? Who were the lecturers?
- Are any of those people widely recognized as national or international leaders in your field? By whom?

Sample questions—lecturing and publications:

- Have you ever presented a lecture at one of these seminars?
- On what topic?
- How long was your presentation?
- Was there a question and answer session after your presentation? How long was that session?
- Have you lectured to any other groups on subjects relating to document examination? Who? When?
- What publications do you recognize as being valuable in your field?
- Do you subscribe to these publications?
- Have any of your own articles been published? When?
- Has your work been published in any national periodical publications? Which ones?
- Have you authored any books or sections of books, relating to document examination?

Sample questions—graphology:

- Have you ever studied the field of graphology or graphoanalysis?
- Do you accept any of the claims made for these methods?

Graphology Is Not a Credential

Persons whose only study of handwriting examination has been through a mail-order or short-term course in graphology are sometimes brought to the witness stand as handwriting experts. The attorney faced with such a witness must make it clear to the court that such studies are not relevant to forensic document examination.

There are several schools of thought in the area of graphology. Each believes itself to be the best method of analyzing handwriting to gain personality insights. Each school of thought has its supporters who claim theirs to be the true and scientific approach to personality assessment.

The attorney who must cross-examine a graphologist who comes to the witness stand as an expert need not get caught in a word game. For the following questions use the noun or verb the witness chooses.

- Are you certified as a graphologist, or some synonymous title?
- If so, by what group?
- Does that certification relate explicitly to forensic document examination, or, does it in anyway relate to personality analysis?
- What courses in graphology have you studied?
- Who produced these courses?
- How long did it take you to complete the course?
- Was the course you completed conducted as a mail-order or correspondence course?
- How much of that course dealt specifically with forensic document examination? (If conducting a deposition, ask the witness to supply copies of the sections of the course relating to document examination for the record.)
- Have you attended seminars for graphologists?
- Did those seminars offer any classes restricted to the study of document examination?
- How long was the seminar?
- How long was the class on document examination? (If conducting a deposition, request that copies of the seminar schedule including topics, lecture times, and the names of teachers be provided for the record.)
- How much of that course dealt with personality and character descriptions?
- Do you believe that a person who writes large will be more outgoing than a person who writes small?
- Do you believe a person who slants the writing to the right is more emotional than one who writes a vertical hand?
- Do you believe that a person who makes extra hooks or loops in the letters *a* or *o* is apt to be misleading or dishonest with others?

In response to this line of questioning, many graphologists will explain that the interpretation of handwriting as a reflection of personality requires extensive "evaluation." Evaluation implies that some specific formulas are employed to reach the final assessment of a trait. Challenge the witness to produce any published formulas or criteria that could be used in such evaluations.

- Do you agree that questioned document examination is a field that requires the practitioner to be disciplined in the scientific method?
- Do you agree that sound scientific practice would include conducting an open-minded study of all sides of a question?
- Have you read or studied any of the research that indicates graphology does not work? Which studies have you read?
- If you have read them—do you agree, or disagree, with the researchers conclusions?
- Can you cite even one independent, scientifically sound study that supports these claims? Is that study published in a recognized, independent journal?
- How can you claim to be an objective scientist in the area of handwriting examination and still accept claims, relevant to handwriting examination, that have been repeatedly proven invalid by scientific testing?

Cross-Examination on Working Methods and Judgments

The next area to attack on cross-examination are the working methods of the examiner and the judgments the examiner made about the case in the process of reaching an opinion. Questioning should explore how the examiner defined the universe of possible writers, on what criteria the examiner ranked the individuality of the questioned and exemplar materials, how the examiner arrived at the definition of the subject's range of normal variation, what tests the examiner completed that support a conclusive opinion, and on what bases the examiner decided any differences are either insignificant or explainable.

Challenging an Expert's Negative Findings

When the expert being examined has reached the opinion that *Q* does *not* match *K* (a negative finding), the judgments made and the methods used to conduct the examination must be cross-examined on behalf of the parties interested in proving that *Q* and *K* are, in fact, by the same person. The attorney hopes to show that the examiner on the witness stand has reached a false negative finding.

False negative findings in signature cases may result from an error in judging the significance of some elemental difference seen in the questioned signature. If the difference on which the examiner is basing the negative opinion is an isolated, elemental one (Figure One), it is quite possible the opinion is wrong. The following questions will help an attorney cross-examine an expert on the possibility of a false negative opinion.

• Did the subject signature show indications of pen speed equal to that defined by this person's exemplars?

• Did the subject signature show proportions at least roughly equal to those defined by this person's exemplars?

• Did the subject signature show pen pressure and patterns of changing pressure equal to what is defined by the exemplars?

• Did the subject signature show character designs which are like those seen in the exemplar signatures?

• How many exemplar signatures were you given?

• Of that number, how many did you select as being sufficient to define the writer's range of normal variation?

• Therefore, if we look at the exemplars you did *not* select for inclusion in your analysis, we should not find any variation not included in the definition of normal variations you have developed? (At this point in the cross-examination the expert's response will lead to one of two paths of questioning:

1) If an exemplar not included in your analysis shows some variation of writing habit you failed to consider, then isn't it possible that other exemplars would include the small points you are now calling significant differences?

Or

2) Since you had to include every signature available to you in your analysis, isn't it very likely that if you had more exemplar signatures you would find a broader definition of the subject's range of normal variation, including, of course, the variation that is the basis for the negative finding?)

The cross-examination might proceed as follows:

• If that is true (either the expert needed more signatures to reach a full definition of normal variations, or the expert excluded a signature that shows a variation not in the definition of variations used for the final study), then isn't it also true that this minor difference, which is the basis for your negative opinion, might also be found in some other exemplar?

• If this difference were to be found in even one genuine signature, then that would change your definition of this writer's range of normal variation, would it not? Therefore, the questioned signature would then match the defined habits of this writer? And, if the questioned signature matched the *fully defined* habits for this writer, your opinion would be reversed. Isn't that correct?

• Is every signature that you or I make perfectly produced?

• Can you, or I, or this subject, experience a handwriting accident or a one-time-only variation in the processes that underlie signing our names?

• If you experienced a once-in-a-life-time interruption in the flow of your signature, would you then expect an expert, such as yourself, to come into court and declare that signature to be a forgery?

False negative opinions can also be caused by accepting contrived writings as exemplars. Contrived or disguised writing standards may come into the case as request standards. To avoid being misled by disguised exemplars, the examiner should have taken three steps.

First, the examiner should have requested a large volume of exemplars. It is very difficult to maintain a disguise through a large volume of material.

Second, the examiner should have repeated the process of taking request exemplars a few weeks after taking the first set. The first and second sets of request exemplars should have been compared. It is very difficult for someone to reproduce a disguise after some time has past. For both sets of exemplars, the subject should have been instructed to write slowly and clearly, to write at normal writing speed, and to write hurriedly. (The examiner must try to get Careful, Common, and Careless writings—not only Contrived writings.)

And, third, the examiner should have insisted on searching out at least one example of the suspect's normal-course-of-business writing. Any writing from before the time frame of the questioned material would help establish the validity of the writing habits as defined by the request exemplars.

• How much exemplar writing did you take from this suspect?

• Did you take exemplar writings from this person on more than one occasion?

• Why not?

• Did you search for any normal-course-of-business writings to include in your reference base?

• Did you search for a driver's license? A mortgage or deed? A voter registration card? Checks? Bank accounts? School work? Medical records?

• Did you ask for any letters or cards sent to friends or relatives?

• Without some earlier writings you had to assume the material produced at your request was not disguised. Isn't it true that some people have more than one way to write?

• Isn't it true that for some people, writing style varies a great deal, depending on how much care is taken with it?

• How can you be certain you are not looking at differences that are the result of intentional effort to write in a different style?

Challenging an Expert's Positive Findings

In this scenario counsel must cross-examine an expert who has offered the opinion that a questioned signature is authentic (*Q* matches *K*). It is in the client's interest to prove that the subject signature is not authentic.

Many false-positive opinions are the result of an examiner failing to recognize how easily the signature involved might be forged. If the signature in question displays only quick rhythmic simple pen movements, or slowly written simple forms, or a collection of exemplar signatures shows a great range of variation, then questions will be posed regarding the degree of individuality in the questioned material. Such questions would be:

• Do you believe the signature in question in this case shows unique handwriting habits? What are they?

• Are you saying that no one else could write at this speed?

• Or, are you saying that no one else could produce these simple forms?

• Isn't it true that many people have a writing style very much like this?

• Couldn't someone with a sharp eye and a desire to produce this simple signature succeed after a little practice?

When the subject's exemplars define an unusually wide range of normal variation, any forger would have a relatively easy task. Questions which would bring this point out could include:

• Isn't it true that by comparing almost any one of the subject's true signatures with the rest of the exemplars, you find some noticeable differences?

• If a forger wanted to imitate this subject's signature, wouldn't the forger have to make some gross, obvious mistakes before the forgery would show any variations not included in the subject's own signatures?

• Wouldn't you expect that a forger, with a little practice, might be able to write a signature that matches one or another of these widely varying exemplars? Or, at least, not make a mistake any greater than the differences we see in these exemplars?

If the universe of possible writers was defined as very small or, as is often the case, limited to a universe of one, then a likely cause of error would be that the examiner has overestimated the importance of common writing habits that happen to be found in both the questioned and exemplar material. As in a physical identification based on common characteristics, if writings from more persons were also examined, others would be found that also match on those same points.

• Are you familiar with the term "universe of possible writers"? Please explain that term for us.

• In this case, how was the universe of possible writers defined? By whom? Did you agree with that definition?

• How large did you consider the universe of possible writers to be?

• Looking only at the writing habits depicted in the questioned materials, how individualized do you believe these writing habits to be?

• Would you, as an experienced expert, say these writing habits would be found in only one writing in 2 million?

• In 1 million? In 100,000? In 10,000? In 1000? In 100?

• Specifically, what makes you think this writing is so unusual, that only one person in ____ could possibly have produced it?

If the signature in question does appear to be genuine, the cross-examination can raise the possibility of a highly skilled forgery. For example:

• Isn't it possible for a forger to learn to sign names with a natural writing style? That is, without slow, trembling hands?

• If a spouse, or a secretary, frequently signs someone else's name, would each of those signatures show the typical slow pen speed or so-called, tremor of forgery?

• Then is it possible for someone to sign or forge, another's name without that signature showing slow, unsteady pen movements or retouching?

If the expert's opinion depends on some explanation of why the questioned signature is different from the exemplars, the opposing counsel needs to cross-examine vigorously for the validity of that reason. The expert should be challenged to cite validated research to support the explanation being offered. This line of questioning might proceed as follows:

- You have said the signature in question includes some movements that are not found in the exemplars. You have said that you accept (fill in the reason) as the cause for these differences, and that with the differences thus explained, you believe the signature to be authentic. What specific research can you cite to support your theory that ___________ would cause this variation in handwriting movement?
- Where is that research published?
- If that theory is your own, what research data do you have to support your theory?
- When did you do that study?
- How was your study controlled?
- Who has repeated your research, and what was the outcome of that work? Where is that study published?

Expert witnesses from many disciplines have been criticized as being hired guns and worse. Some of that criticism has been warranted. Some has not. When professional witnesses express poorly grounded opinions and those opinions go unchallenged, who is at fault? Yes, the expert is ethically and morally wrong. But, what about the attorney who failed to impeach that testimony?

For the legal system to work, attorneys need to hire honest experts who can explain their work in understandable terms. And, attorneys need to do the homework necessary to effectively cross-examine opposing experts.

Chapter Fifteen

CREDENTIALS—TRAINING AND CERTIFICATION

It would seem that a discussion of the training of a handwriting expert would come at the beginning of this book. However, by now the reader has some understanding of the work of a handwriting expert. With an understanding of the disciplines and skills necessary to be effective in this work, it is easier to understand how to acquire these tools.

Document examination requires an integration of a wide range of skills—some technical and some personal. Document examination employs the scientific method and the thinking processes of scientific inquiries. An examiner must be objective, open-minded, and work in a systematic, thorough manner. Document examiners learn the disciplined use of the tools of science, but signature examination is not a science.[48]

The work of a document examiner is a technical discipline, requiring learning how to observe details and follow a disciplined thinking process, analyze information, and interpret the results of tests and measurements. Document examiners are routinely called upon to do exacting, technical work—they are not called upon to do brain surgery, launch moon shots, or split atoms. Anyone with an aptitude and appetite for technical work can master the technical aspects of document examination. I agree with Ordway Hilton, author of *Scientific Examination of Questioned Documents,* "The most important qualification of a witness is his ability to do the work."[49]

A document examiner makes critical decisions. It is common for a case to either go forward or to end, depending on the document examiner's findings. Each case must be handled correctly so as not to damage the value of the evidence involved. Handwriting examinations must be properly organized and the comparisons systematically carried out. If

[48]Conway, p. 57.

[49]Hilton, p. 405.

other testing, such as comparisons of inks or developing indented images, becomes necessary, these tests must be done with the correct technical methods and skills. Some work, such as chemical analysis of inks, is highly specialized and requires costly equipment and expertise beyond that of the general document examiner. When such work is needed, the document examiner should refer that work to a specialized laboratory. In signature examination cases, the document examiner's most important work is done at the desk and in the courtroom, not in the laboratory.

The best experts are able to balance a mixture of scientific thinking, teaching, and salesmanship. The examiner must have the technical disciplines necessary to arrive at the correct answers, but being correct is not enough. The true measure of an expert's value is taken in the courtroom, in front of a jury. The examiner must be able to inform jurors and persuade them of the correctness of the opinions being offered. If the expert is "too scientific," the jury won't get it—"too slick" or arrogant, and the jury won't like it.

A small handful of adjectives describes what an attorney is looking for when hiring an expert. Mature, confident, articulate and accurate in both the written and spoken word, comfortable with public speaking, inquisitive, thick-skinned, and patient would cover the most important personal traits. A general knowledge of the legal system, familiarity with the scientific method, and thorough, specific knowledge of forensic document examination cover the technical requirements.

How does one acquire these tools? Who are the teachers? Many of the traits and skills listed above are acquired through general education. Maturity, self-confidence, patience, and the strength to weather a critical attack are qualities that are built throughout life. Competence with written and spoken language comes from education and practice. Public speaking skills are only acquired by speaking in public. The best way to gain the educational and personal experiences that develop these traits is through a good college education. However, no college offers degree programs in handwriting identification or document examination.

So, what courses should be in the curriculum for a student who wishes to become a document examiner? The basic curriculum should have an emphasis on writing skills, visual arts, critical thinking, and public speaking. The student needs to be familiar with the scientific method and logical problem solving. Courses in physics, mathematics, and basic computer programming will develop technical thinking skills and provide a useful base of knowledge. Courses covering investigative methods and evidence handling will also be valuable.

Communications skills and the foundation knowledge that will be needed can be developed through college courses. While many of the leading document examiners, past and present, gained training and experience through apprenticeships and have not completed college, it would be foolhardy to try to start this career today without the benefits of a college education. In this age, to try to get the courts to accept a young person without a degree as an expert would be asking too much. Can one have all of the skills necessary to do first-rate work without a degree? Yes, document examination is not a hard science nor is it a licensed profession. It is possible to become a first-rate examiner without a college degree; many have done so, but it is a harder path.

With a basic education completed, acquiring the necessary specialized knowledge will still be difficult. Examiners who train through affiliation with a government laboratory will have the luxury of being paid while they study. Anyone wishing to work in private practice will need to work harder than their government counterpart in order to acquire the necessary knowledge.

Most examiners who have trained privately have done so while holding down other jobs to support themselves. What can be learned in a year or two of on-the-job training can also be learned in four or five years of dedicated self-study.

There are technical associations offering workshops and useful lectures at their annual meetings. Technical associations offering certification testing may also offer study guidelines and information as to resources for books, articles, and equipment. Some students are fortunate to have found a skilled mentor to guide their studies. Whether working in a government lab or working alone, the techniques and skills needed to work as a document examiner must be developed through self-study.

Many independent students searching for training in forensic handwriting examination enroll in courses offering training in "handwriting analysis." In the United States the term handwriting analysis has come to be synonymous with the practices of graphology. Courses in graphology teach the theory that personality and even character are projected in handwriting habits. There is an old adage which holds that a half-truth is more dangerous than a lie. In my opinion, that adage applies to this subject.

Do many flamboyant, outgoing people have a writing style that is large with long pen movements and flourishes? Yes. Do many people who are detail-oriented and reserved, write in a small, perhaps uniformly printed style? Yes. Do many teenage girls write in a round, so called "bubble" style? Again, yes.

There is little reason to doubt that an overall writing style can be somewhat reflective of personal taste—similar to choice of dress and body language. European document examiners study the overall relationships between writing style and the other personality projections. They also recognize that these relationships between writing style and personality have low levels of reliability and significance. Many people may reflect something of their general personality in their general writing style. The courses in handwriting analysis assume that closer study of a subject's writing equates with a closer study of the subject's personality. In that step, the half-truth becomes a lie.

Theories of graphology have been taught for decades. Numerous well-designed, independent studies of these theories and of the effectiveness of their practitioners have been conducted. Self-serving studies aside, no independently conducted, scientifically sound study has yet reported a significantly positive correlation between the details of handwriting habits and personality.

For the student of forensic handwriting examination, courses in graphology are of little value. Any practice in studying handwriting is useful, but it is not necessary to pay for a course in unproven personality correlations when one's purpose is to study handwriting in minute detail. I believe that document examiners who practice or support the claims made for graphology diminish their value to their questioned document clients.

Of course, it is possible to be knowledgeable and skilled in more than one discipline; that is not the issue. How can juries find an expert credible when that expert supports theories of personality projection in handwriting which have been repeatedly discredited by the scientific method? No matter how skillfully and accurately a forensic examination of handwritings is conducted, the findings are of value to the client only when that examiner can serve as a credible witness. If one is going to attempt to defend unscientific theories of graphology, a skilled attorney will reveal nonscience to be nonsense by the time that witness leaves the stand.

There is a need for well-designed training programs in this field. Currently, this need is being addressed only through self-study and by some correspondence courses, which may or may not teach the necessary skills. In this situation, why don't colleges offer curriculums in document examination? There are two answers to that question.

First, it is a matter of supply and demand. While only a few dedicated persons have kept themselves motivated enough to develop successful private practices, in the private sector there is not a shortage of document examiners. Police departments and government agencies who have document labs are able to train the personnel they need to keep themselves staffed. Thus, if a college graduated a class of examiners, they would have a tough time finding work or building their own businesses.

Second, at least in the area of handwriting examination, there has been no logical, clearly teachable method. Each examiner has picked up bits of technique and information from more experienced examiners and each has developed an individualized working method from the basic building blocks given to us by pioneers such as Osborn and Harrison. If an examiner is also a talented teacher, a do-as-I-do, on-the-job apprentice training program can work to teach one student at a time, but it cannot support a classroom of students.

Ironically, in the government sector, where some training is available, there is a shortage of document examiners. In many areas, even large police departments do not have a qualified examiner. And, training an examiner becomes a catch-22 situation.

In the current teaching model, an examiner can only be trained in a department that already has an experienced examiner. The thinking is that a trainee must work side-by-side with a mentor for two years before working independently. Departments without an examiner cannot afford to send someone to another city for two years of training.

A student with a good foundation in the scientific method, an interest in technical subjects, and good communication skills can become a qualified examiner without having to relocate for two years. Through self-study, participation in seminars and basic workshops presented by professional associations, and with help from a mentor via phone, computer, and fax, a student can become proficient while maintaining a regular work schedule. At least one professional association makes meaningful written and oral examinations for certification available to independent students.

Certification

Document examination is not a licensed profession. There are no formal degrees offered through the regular degree programs of colleges or universities. (A few examiners have completed degrees in document examination through "design your own degree programs.") Without degrees or licenses, there are a number of professional associations which offer certification. Certification offers the courts or the hiring attorney a credential to show that an expert's knowledge and skills are recognized by a peer group. There are several groups which offer certification and it seems that a new group is started every year or two. Obviously not all certifications have the same value.

What are the parameters of a meaningful certification program? Certification ought to give the legal profession a reliable indication that the examiner has the knowledge and skills necessary to serve the legal system. An attorney hiring a certified document examiner should feel confident that the person will conduct an open-minded, independent examination of the evidence and report the results accurately. When called for, the examiner must be able to write a clear and accurate report, build quality exhibits, and present convincing testimony. Every aspect of the examiner's work should reflect a high level of ethics and professionalism.

A good certification program incorporates the following elements:

- Written examinations based on recognized texts.
- Oral examinations conducted by a panel of experienced examiners.
- Testing done in a monitored environment.
- Testing completed within a reasonable time. (Not done at home over a period of days or weeks.)
- Testing which includes working on practical case problems.
- A process which involves attorneys and/or judges who are not members of the group to review the applicant's work.
- A process which involves lay persons in the role of jurors to review the applicant's presentation of a case.
- Periodic proficiency testing and/or participation at educational seminars as requirements to maintain certification.
- A good certification program is open to anyone wishing to sit for the examinations without requiring membership in that particular group. It tests what you know—not who you know.

Persons who have passed written tests, sat for oral examinations and had their work reviewed by a lay jury, as well as by legal professionals, have gone to great lengths to establish a meaningful credential for their skills.

A good certification program does not include:

- Grandfather clauses that bypass certification testing.
- Certification that does not require proficiency testing and/or continuing education.
- Certification that is only granted in conjunction with membership in that association.
- Tests in which the questions are so simplistic they make the process a test in name only.
- Tests mailed out to be completed at home.
- Tests done with open books, without monitoring, or without time limits.

Unfortunately, there are many groups offering rather meaningless certification for document examiners. Membership in, or even certification by, any group does not automatically equate with skill and knowledge. Some groups are closed to all but government-trained examiners. Some groups rely on member referrals to admit new examiners. Some groups rely on objective testing of the applicant's skills. And, some groups are willing to offer credentials to anyone wishing to apply. All of these groups consist of both talented and marginally capable examiners. An attorney needing to hire an examiner cannot rely solely on association membership or certification by any peer group as full assurance of the examiner's abilities. This shouldn't be surprising as even membership in the bar does not guarantee the skills of an attorney.

At times, the political wrangling among examiners from different backgrounds becomes ugly. At its worst, some examiners may offer a "second opinion" to support a "fraternity brother" rather than conduct their own independent, open-minded, objective examination. Such poor practices cause all document examiners to appear less professional than they are.

Document examiners work in the legal environment where the advocacy system puts them to the most meaningful test possible. When an attorney needs to hire a document examiner the best first step is to request references. Talk with attorneys who have used the expert in their own cases and with attorneys who have encountered that expert working for their opposition. Any document examiner worth considering will provide those references. A candid conversation with attorneys who have first-hand experience with the expert being considered will be more informative than anyone's curriculum-vitae.

In the end, it is best that the decision whether or not any examiner is found to be qualified and credible is left to the judge and jury. They are best positioned and best equipped to decide who is an expert. They are also best qualified to decide whether the opinions and reasoning of an expert make sense.

By practicing a consistent set of working standards and ethics, doing skillful work, and making credible presentations of evidence, the talented examiner will establish a positive reputation.

To Begin Studying Questioned Document Examination

Cases in which the validity of a signature is questioned are the most frequent reason for hiring a document examiner. That is why this book was written. To begin a study of document examination it makes sense to begin by studying signatures.

The first step for a student is to build a reference library. Books on document examination are not best sellers and some books listed are out of print. Copies might be found through rare book shops. Many of these books can be found in good law libraries. A law library will also afford the student access to journals such as the *Journal for the Association of Forensic Document Examiners* (available on West Law) and the *Journal of the Academy of Forensic Sciences.*

As recommended in Chapter One, begin to build a collection of study materials. Collect two or three dozen old checks from several friends. Enlarge the signatures and mount them on study boards. Observe the range of variation for each of the elements of comparison and make notes of those variations.

Go back to those friends and ask them to produce forged signatures of each other's names. For each name, request simple forgeries, tracings, and simulations. These materials will provide you with your own illustrations and examples to study when you reread this book and study the other books and articles in your library.

Have your friends produce blind tests for you. These test situations should include a questioned signature, which might include contrived changes or might be forged, and a set of exemplars.

Forensic signature examination is a discipline which is acquired in the same manner as any other discipline. Study the literature and practice the methods so that they become second nature.

Document examiners must master many skills other than signature examination. Handwriting identification, working on cases which involve numbers or printing and all of the techniques relating to physical testing will eventually be studied. For the new student, signature examination should come first.

If you have read this book thoroughly, you know the basic structure of the discipline you will be learning. Now, collect your study materials and begin again. As you study this book apply the techniques presented here to the materials in your own collection. Take time with each step. Apply the techniques to as many sample situations as you can. Expect to spend several months practicing and developing the skills needed.

Discipline is just that—discipline. Patiently take each step one at a time and in order. Resist jumping to any conclusion about a signature. You will build a good foundation for later studies by patiently practicing the scientific method as it applies to forensic signature examination.

BIBLIOGRAPHY

Baker, J. Newton: *Law of Disputed and Forged Documents.* Charlottesville, The Michie Company, 1955.

Conway, James V.P.: *Evidential Documents,* Third Printing. Springfield, Charles C Thomas, 1978.

Harrison, Wilson R.: *Forgery Detection, A Practical Guide.* New York, Frederick A. Praeger, 1964.

Harrison, Wilson R.: *Suspect Documents, Their Scientific Examination.* Chicago, Nelson-Hall, 1981.

Hilton, Ordway: *Scientific Examination of Questioned Documents,* Revised Edition. New York, Elsevier North Holland, 1982.

Osborn, Albert S.: *Questioned Documents,* Second Edition. Chicago, Nelson-Hall, 1929.

Robertson, Edna W.: *Fundamentals of Document Examination.* Chicago, Nelson-Hall, 1991.

Scott, Charles C.: *Photographic Evidence, Preparation and Presentation,* Second Edition. St. Paul, West, 1969.

Slyter, Steven A.: *Volume 29, American Jurisprudence, Proof of Facts, Third Series.* "The Effects of Alterations to Documents" Pages 549 through 601; Rochester, Lawyers Cooperative Publishing, 1995.

INDEX

U

V

W